Me and that Asperger Kid

A. Teacher

ISBN: 1470165767
ISBN 13: 9781470165765

Library of Congress Control Number: 2013903538

Available for purchase at Amazon.com, Kindle, www.createspace.com/3799797, and other online retailers

www.meandthataspergerkid.com

Dedication

— To teachers everywhere who deal daily with the challenges their students present—with little or no help from the educational establishment.

— To the families of children with autism—hope floats. Many people love and will help your child.

— To those who suffer with this syndrome—stay the course. You bring out the best in others.

— To my real Evan—thank you for being my teacher.

Attributes & Aspects
of Autism

A   udacious

U   nique

T   enacious

I   nquisitive

S   olitary

M   emorable

CONTENTS

Prologue

Those unfamiliar with the workings of a public school system might assume that the placement of a child with Asperger syndrome, a form of autism, into my fifth-grade regular-education class was done in a highly professional manner. Such a first-time placement was probably preceded by at least one meeting with all the school-building professionals involved; perhaps a consultation with an expert in autism had been scheduled. Certainly there was a meeting with the parents and discussions with the child's previous teacher. At the very least, it might be reasoned, the principal would have mentioned the child's placement to the affected teacher.

Those who are familiar with the workings of public schools can readily relate to the fact that I was informed I would be getting a student with this syndrome while on bus duty in the gym, supervising the dismissal of two hundred noisy children.

This child's fourth-grade teacher happened to spot me as she was dropping off her students who take the bus, and she casually told me this information. As I knew almost nothing about Asperger syndrome at the time, except that it was a form of autism, I inquired as to why I would be getting this student. I'd assumed that any student with autism was placed in an inclusion class where additional services are provided. I knew I would never be teaching such a class, as my feelings about the dubious benefits of inclusion as a one-size-fits-all remedy were well known. And this student was, after all, in her fourth-grade inclusion class, so why would he be placed in my regular-education class for fifth grade?

I had no sooner posed this question when a first-grade girl who had a galloping case of "all-the-other-first-graders-are-out-to-get-me" paranoia (worse than my ninety-one-year-old mother's) ran up to me. She tightly wrapped her arms around my waist, knocking me slightly backward burying her face in my clothing. "That's why," said the fourth-grade teacher; then she quickly disappeared.

Having spent thirty-six years of my life as a teacher in public schools, I filed this information into one of the many fuzzy file folders in the back of my brain. Too many things change over the summer for me to worry about something that might not be the case come September. I did, however, inquire informally about Asperger syndrome at an international education society meeting in Iceland that summer—but the fellow members I spoke to seemed to know very little about how to *best* reach and teach a child with this condition.

So, it was with the sum total of my limited and antiquated knowledge of autism—autistic kids rock back and forth, hate to be touched, and are mentally retarded—that I met Evan on the first day of school.

CHAPTER 1

First Impressions: Cute, Charming, Controlling

WELCOME TO FIFTH GRADE – DAY 1

On September 3, Evan bounded into my classroom, talking rapidly and aloud to no one in particular. He chose a seat next to a rather large boy who, I later learned, was one of the smartest boys in the school district. Apparently, Evan had sought out his intellectual equal.

The only thing that separated Evan from the other fifth-graders on that first day was his speech pattern. Here was a cute, blond, blue-eyed little imp who talked in complex sentences and used vocabulary words worthy of a college professor. So much for retardation!

Oh, there were a few monumental clashes those first days because—like Evan—I too am a control freak. As the teacher I felt that was my privilege; but then, so did Evan. However, it didn't take him long to wrap me around his little finger, as I found him to be utterly charming. One thing that I discovered early on about Evan—and maybe Asperger syndrome, too—was that Evan wanted to be in control, but as soon as he gained control of whatever he was fixating on, he almost immediately went on to something else. It was going to be an interesting year, because I kept forgetting this.

OH NO, A LETTER!

As I wanted to form my own impressions of Evan, I waited on contacting his parents. On the ninth day of school, they contacted me. I dreaded opening the letter they sent in with Evan. Experience had taught me that such introductory letters were typically very condescending. They usually intimated that the teacher knew nothing about the special condition their child had. But then, I actually didn't know anything about Asperger syndrome, and, surprisingly, this letter was different. In fact, it set the tone for a positive relationship.

From the beginning, it was the kind of relationship that teachers dream of establishing with parents. Such collaborative relationships don't usually survive because of turf issues and the fact that the teacher's role is that of "pusher" and the parent's role is that of "nurturer."

I came to depend on Evan's dad not only to guide me but also to let me vent. Neither his parents nor I tried to be Monday-morning quarterbacks. This enabled me to be open and honest with them about my short-comings and frustrations in dealing with Evan. I've always felt guilty because I was unable to give them more than six hours of custodial respite. Oh, teaching and learning was going on at school, but so much of the skills' practice, those pencil-on-paper tasks, fell to Dad to complete with Evan at home. Thus, even our roles switched at times, with Evan's dad becoming the pusher and me, his teacher, the nurturer.

WHY ME?

In their introductory letter, Evan's parents said the fact that I had been chosen to be Evan's teacher spoke volumes as to the personality I must have to handle special children. Oh, there was a reason I was given Evan, but I seriously doubted that it was because I was a good teacher or because of my ability to handle special kids. I tend to ruffle feathers and do things my way. I've always been outspoken about current fads and what I found that worked and didn't work in education vis-à-vis a student's needs. So why Evan?

Some of my colleagues thought it might be the school district's way of getting the parents to agree to have Evan classified as a special-education student. But when I asked Evan's parents to allow Evan to be evaluated, they readily agreed.

Although Evan was medically diagnosed with Asperger syndrome and ADHD (attention-deficit/hyperactivity disorder), he was never classified as a student in need of special-education services. Yet he had always been placed in inclusion-type classes in the past.

Inclusion classes in my school building were made up of regular-education students and their teacher, with classified special-education students sprinkled (or sometimes packed) in. A part-time special-education teacher and a teaching assistant were also provided. The part-time special-education teacher was there to modify and clarify the regular curriculum, and the teaching assistant was there to provide continuity when the special-education teacher was elsewhere.

It may sound like a good model, but I'm not sure how well it worked. My misgivings came from the fact that the class was not truly shared with the special-education teacher, who functioned more like a highly skilled specialist and consultant. I was told this happened because the special-education teacher was shared between two classes. Doing this saved the district money.

I was startled to learn that my request for a psychological evaluation was not the first one; so much for my colleagues' theory. It seemed because Evan was such an extremely *bright* boy who scored highly on intelligence and achievement tests that he didn't fit the overriding criterion for special-education services or placement. (By using this one criterion, Helen Keller wouldn't have qualified for special education, either.)

This did not make sense to me, because Evan did exhibit, to varying degrees, not only the symptoms associated with Asperger syndrome but also obsessive and opposition-defiant behaviors. I observed Evan's intense fixations; narrow interests and preoccupations; inappropriate emotional, social, and sexual reactions; repetitive physical behaviors such as twirling, high-pitched shrieking, groaning and growling; trouble with organizational skills; coordination and fine-motor-skill problems; language peculiarities; and (most of all) control issues.

LIKING OTHERS

If I hadn't received a letter from Evan's parents so quickly, I would have had to contact them anyway. It seemed that Evan liked Valarie, a girl in my class, but was clueless about how to show her that he liked her. Somehow this resulted in his being accused of trying to pull down her slacks in the cafeteria during lunch. It wasn't something Evan tried to deny. When I spoke to him privately following the incident, he just said, "I like her." After a chat with the principal, his story was sanitized. In the non-Freudian version, he claimed that Valarie was about to fall down and he was just trying to help her stay upright. I liked his original, straightforward explanation better.

Knowing how to show others you like them should be part of the fifth-grade emerging-sexuality health curriculum. Following this incident, when I suggested to my colleagues at a Child Study Team meeting that we should invite a speaker to a special fifth-grade assembly to discuss boy-girl relationships and the importance of romance, they wanted to know if their husbands could attend, too.

Valarie also spoke with the principal and later to me. She said that she knew Evan was "special" (probably the principal's word) and that he'd liked her since third grade. She was very understanding, and since I never heard anything from her parents about the incident, I guess it was handled appropriately.

The principal said she called Evan's parents and spoke at length with his dad. I also called his dad and gave him Evan's original version. Thus, I wasn't surprised the next day when Evan said that he wanted to give Valarie a note. Of course, I assumed that it was a note of apology. Wrong! The note said, "I hate you!"

As a teacher, I also assumed that a student who got in trouble with his classmates, the adult lunchroom monitors, his teacher, the principal, and his parents would be somewhat subdued the following day. Wrong again! At the morning assembly, Evan told the special-area teacher, who was watching my class, that he was poking his classmates because "I'm obsessive compulsive. I need to poke people. I have issues."

LIKING EVAN

As I stated, Evan and I hit it off from day one. He was extremely intelligent and usually remorseful following behavioral outbursts. Most of the time, I recognized that it was the syndrome that got the better of his good intentions. There were, of course, days when his behaviors grated on my last nerve, especially when he continued to argue his point directly into my ear. (He could easily do this as I am "vertically challenged," being under five feet and shrinking.) Evan also had a great sense of humor (a character trait that I prized in my students), and when we had a clash of wills, whoever won didn't normally use it to their advantage in the next go-round.

Most of his peers liked him, too. If they didn't, they would never have put up with his antics. Evan's needs and behavioral outbursts took a tremendous amount of my time away from them. Whenever Evan felt he needed my attention, he would just interrupt. It didn't matter if I was teaching a lesson, talking to another student, proctoring a test, or interacting with adults. If I was not in the classroom, he would seek me out. His needs were paramount. When he came up to my desk—often throwing his body across my desk blotter—those students waiting to talk to me would walk away. Luckily, I noticed this early on in the school year, and I told them, in no uncertain terms, that they were to wait for me to finish with Evan. There was no putting him off, but they were important, too.

THE MUSIC TEACHER

Although my first impressions of Evan were undeniably positive, it wasn't the same for the music teacher. They didn't hit it off. It was toward the end of September when this teacher, a second-year rookie, came to get me. Our rooms were almost opposite each other, and I had known this teacher back when she was a student in our middle school. She told me that Evan was being uncooperative and that his behavior was preventing her from teaching the class. Really? Imagine that!

I went immediately to collect him. Although I stood at the door and beckoned to him, he ignored me. This had nothing to do with a lack of understanding social cues, poor eye contact, or an inability to read my facial expression. We had solid eye contact and he knew exactly what I wanted, but his facial expression and body language conveyed that he intended to stay put. Therefore, I walked over to him, firmly grasped his hand, and led him from the classroom. He didn't resist me physically, and once back in our classroom he busied himself with his current fixation.

The principal somehow found out about this incident and told me that I had handled it all wrong. (What else is new?) According to her, I should have taken the rest of the class back to my room when Evan refused to budge, leaving him alone in the music room. (When I got advice like this, I'd seriously consider the positive aspects of retirement. Had Evan been placed in my class for just this reason?)

To make sure that I was on the same page as Evan's dad, I called him. He thought he would have handled the situation in the same way and was only upset because Evan had given two of his teachers a hard time.

As the year progressed, Evan, who enjoyed singing and loved dancing, continued procrastinating when it was time to go to music class. He'd have a million things that he needed to do first. Finally, it just became easier to let him stay with me. He had to work quietly, as it was my prep period and I had lots of things that I needed to accomplish. I knew I could trust him in the room by himself if I had to dash to the lavatory. If I needed to make a phone call or attend a meeting, I'd urge him to go to music class and promise to pick him up early, if possible.

OTHER TEACHERS

It was during one of these time periods when a third-grade teacher, whose classroom was next to mine, came looking for an older student to keep an eye on her class in case she needed to dash somewhere (the lavatory being the unspoken destination). Evan's ears perked up upon hearing this request, because he loved supervising younger students. He was just oozing charm and charisma when he told her that he would be glad to help her out.

He had volunteered earlier in the year to help a first-grade teacher get a group of her students to their bus at dismissal time. He wanted to quit after a harrowing first day, but I insisted he stick with it. I told him that when I was a first-grade teacher, I had considered quitting after the first day, too. After several weeks, this first-grade teacher reported to me that he was doing an excellent job—that is, except for one day when she was running late and Evan interrupted her lesson to announce in a loud, piercing, imperious voice that his group should line up immediately.

Getting back to the third-grade teacher, she was immediately smitten with Mr. Charm's response to her request. Being the only student in my room at the time certainly hadn't hurt his chances of being picked, but neither this teacher nor any third-grade student in her class ever complained about Evan or questioned his authority or ability to monitor the class. He continued minding her class as needed for the rest of the year.

First impressions are indeed lasting ones!

CHAPTER 2

Brokering Deals;
Fueling Fixations

DEALS TO ASPIRATIONS

Famous TV hosts had nothing on Evan when it came to *Let's Make a Deal*. There's probably a career opportunity here, as Evan could talk the hindquarters off a mule.

At first, I envisioned Evan becoming a documentary filmmaker since he was such a visual learner. But when I got to know him better, I discovered that he wanted to be an attorney. Because arguing and deal-making were as natural for him as breathing, his career choice seemed a valid one. I can still imagine him arguing for our teachers' union—fighting the good fight; I can also imagine him arguing for the other side—scary.

A highly sought-after surgeon once told me that he had to compete with students who had Asperger syndrome in medical school. He thought he'd want someone with Asperger's to operate on him, since those medical students "seemed totally focused." Considering that Evan's intense focus could suddenly evaporate, I was glad he was leaning toward the law.

FUELING FIXATIONS

Evan was at my desk ready to start arguing as soon as I completed writing the daily agenda on the board. Occasionally, some of the activities met with his approval, but more often he had different ideas for the use of his time in class.

In the fall, Evan was obsessed with crossword puzzles. In fact, a young teacher who had substituted for me reported that Evan had been engrossed in a crossword puzzle in *Newsday*. He was amazed that a ten-year-old had been able to complete so much of it. (I was amazed that a teacher smart enough to let Evan design his own learning activity was still substituting.)

What I tried to do was work Evan's current fixation, when appropriate, into his learning routine. If he was into doing crossword puzzles, well, that was his language-arts activity for the day.

SHOCK TREATMENT

Sometimes I had to play Nurse Ratched and shock Evan out of whatever he was fixated on. If I wanted him to participate in a lesson or a checkup of homework, I'd announce in a loud voice, "Evan, get ready to answer number 6!" I was usually sorry I didn't pick on him to answer number 14, because it took him so long to get out his materials and turn to the correct page. But if I had done that, he would have waited until we got to number 13 to comply, and the class would still have had to wait for him.

By allowing him time to work on what he wanted and then purposely interrupting him in some dramatic way, I could also get him to do an example or problem in math, which was his least favorite subject. He complied more readily when I allowed him to work on an example at the blackboard because he liked touching and using chalk. Shaving chalk with his pencil sharpener was one of his favorite repetitive behaviors. (I doubt, however, that I will ever think of a curriculum connection for the hundreds of shards of chalk that had comprised a bed of dust and grime in the bottom of one of the two desks he considered his.)

OUT IN LEFT FIELD

Even though math was Evan's weakest area, he tried fooling around with it. He devised a way to subtract from left to right. Although a few of my former students and one of Evan's current classmates could do it this way, Evan could never fully explain how he was doing it. Thus, I couldn't tell if his errors were due to his refusal to write down how he was regrouping or if it was because of some other flaw in his process. When we began harder multiplication problems, I noticed that he was having difficulty not only with regrouping but also with recalling the more difficult multiplication facts. I checked with his fourth-grade teacher, who by this time probably dreaded another one of my questions. She recalled him knowing all his number facts. When his father happened to stop by my room concerning something else, I asked him if Evan did indeed know all his multiplication tables. He, too, thought that Evan did know them, but said he would review them with him.

In spite of Dad's coaching, Evan continued to experience difficulty. His failure in math would later be the fuel I used to ignite the "powers that be" into providing him (and therefore me) with some help. But I am getting ahead of myself.

HOORAY FOR HOLLYWOOD

The second week of school, while showing an educational video about Egyptian artifacts, I noticed that Evan was mesmerized. I began capitalizing on this teaching method by using films (old tapes and DVDs) to focus his attention on different subjects, topics, and concepts.

I was using the Egyptian film to show how archeologists use artifacts to study cultures. I wanted my students to hear the technical vocabulary these scientists used when talking with their colleagues. Following the film, I planned to give a list of many of the same specialized vocabulary words to my students to memorize. Their assignment would also include collecting and bringing in artifacts that defined them—trophies, medals, games and sports equipment, faux jewelry, Barbie dolls, etc.

With Evan, I had to decide early on whether I would use films as a learning channel or as a reward for completing tasks and demonstrating appropriate behavior; I picked the former. For the latter, I would use the classroom computer.

I could teach the entire fifth-grade social studies curriculum through films, even if I didn't have a student like Evan who thrived on this kind of approach. I've been criticized in the past for doing so, not because it is history according to Hollywood—a valid criticism—but because most administrators see no value in showing films. I think they believe all information must be imparted directly through stand-up lectures or textbooks. Even my students thought they were getting away with something when I scheduled a film. Showing a film must indicate that the teacher is either resting or goofing off. So much for visual learning styles.

COMPUTER GEEK

Evan's love of computer activities enabled me to challenge his abilities in science. I was able to do this by using Bob Ballard's science curriculum, also known as The JASON Project.[1] Each year this curriculum required an investigation of a different biome. One year it focused on the Polar Regions; another year, the Channel Islands; another, Hawaii.

---

1   The JASON Project: JASON Education through Exploration.

For Evan's class, it was Panama and the tropical rain forest on Barro Colorado Island.

The digital labs created by Ballard's team of scientists for this rain forest project were, in my opinion, the best ever. One lab required students to become traffic controllers on the canal. They had to navigate three different types of ships through it. When students did so successfully, they received colorful certificates of achievement. Another lab, "Race to Reforest," required students to play the role of a small landowner who needed to plant trees to prevent intrusive grass from growing, create a source of income, and be environmentally sound.

At the beginning of this unit, Evan completed many labs, but eventually a noninstructional computer game got the better of his attention. However, he came through for me on the day of The JASON Project teleconference.

On this day, students from different schools met at specific sites around the country to show off what they knew and could do, and to ask questions. This teleconference also enabled highly regarded scientists to actually answer students' questions while they continued working on their experiments in the field in Panama.

Teachers were asked to assign students specific tasks to complete before the video portion began. I'd asked Evan to work with the group headed by an adult science technician on the digital labs. I'm sure the only person who realized that Evan was not just another typical, bright fifth-grader was his partner, Matthew. After the teleconference, Matthew complained to me that Evan had pinched him throughout the lab portion. I asked Matt how he had handled it, and he replied, "Finally, I just had to pinch him back."

Since Evan—who bellowed loudly when he felt a classmate had maltreated him—hadn't registered a complaint with me about the pinching, he must've figured that Matthew had handled it correctly.

CHAPTER 3

Surviving Parties

HALLOWEEN

I found that if I could walk Evan through an upcoming party or event, he could handle it. Case in point—Halloween.

I had a reputation among students for throwing "the best" Halloween party, much to the chagrin of building and district administrators. It was one of the first things my students asked me about on the opening day of school.

A typical school party entails eating cupcakes and drinking juice while sitting at a desk for a short period before dismissal. Some teachers allow Halloween costumes, but lately costumes are being outlawed at many grade levels. Instead, students are told that they can wear a T-shirt that is either orange or black. Fun, huh?

The thinking here is to get Halloween over with as quickly as possible. There's not much capitalizing on the students' enthusiasm, except for making jack-o-lanterns and place mats in the lower grades or writing ghost stories in the upper grades

For a holiday that is second only to Christmas in popularity, it certainly gets the short shrift in schools. And this has nothing to do with the religious significance of All Hallows' Eve. In all the years that I hosted Halloween parties, I can only recall one child who wasn't allowed to attend the festivities in my classroom for religious reasons. Her father explained to me in great detail that they were Christians and that Halloween wasn't a Christian holiday. (He did, however, let her attend our Sikh and Hanukkah eat-ins, though I'm not sure if he knew that she also sipped water from Zamzam—the well located within the Masjid al-Haram—and tasted a date and fig that her class-mate brought back from Mecca.)

A former college professor of mine (who later became a principal) told me she had to explain to an irate parent one Halloween morning that we try to teach tolerance, cultural understanding, and, hopefully, acceptance of others by celebrating various holidays. She did this while dressed as a grape.

As my Halloween parties bore little resemblance to those Evan would have been familiar with, I offered a detailed explanation of what would transpire.

Our conversation went something like this:

"First of all, there will be a lot of adults present and noisy preschoolers and crying babies in strollers, as everyone is invited. Make sure your parents know they're invited."

"They can't come. They work."

"Invite them anyhow! You'll change into your costume after lunch."

"I don't eat lunch, but I have a great costume with a mask."

"No masks! After you change, you'll be given a big black plastic bag to put over your head, so you won't get your costume dirty."

"I'll suffocate!"

"The class mother puts a slit in the top of the bag so you can get it over your head and makes slits for your arms, too. *YOU WON'T SUFFOCATE!* After that, we'll go outside and have a raw-egg toss."

"I'll get all gooey."

"EXACTLY!"

"I'll have to wash my hands."

"*THEN*, we'll come back to the classroom, *GET CLEANED UP*, and play musical chairs."

"What about I don't want to play?"

"You can participate in *ALL* the activities, or you can stay home."

"Oh."

"After musical chairs, we'll have an ice cream-eating contest. The parents will put a dish of ice cream with chocolate syrup and whipped cream on each of the chairs we used in the game. When it's your turn, you'll kneel in front of a chair with your hands behind your back and wait for the signal to start eating."

"I don't like chocolate syrup or whipped cream. I don't even like ice cream that much."

"I can tell the class mother not to put any chocolate syrup on yours. Try to eat around and under the whipped cream, as it's all part of the fun. You're supposed to get it all over your face and in your eyes, ears, and up your nose. In fact, some of the fathers will be squirting additional whipped cream into the bowls as you eat. So don't get upset. Your face is supposed to be a mess by the end of the contest."

"I'll have to wash up again. I have to go to the after-school program."

"*AFTER* the winners get their prizes, we'll have the mummy-wrapping contest, so remember to bring in a roll of toilet paper."

"Is that it?"

"Yep!"

"You forgot changing back into my school clothes!"

Needless to say, Evan had a wonderful time at this Halloween party designed especially for kids. The teacher, however, went home exhausted.

OTHER HOLIDAYS

Some of Evan's enthusiasm and party skills carried over to our "Make Your Own Egg Cream" Christmas/Hanukkah party. He readily researched (but grudgingly wrote a brief report about) the history of this New York drink and complied with my directives for actually making one, though he refused to drink it.

He also had a fit because I wouldn't allow him to open his grab-bag gift ahead of time. My students had been reading *The House Without a Christmas Tree,*[2] a novel that deals with father/daughter conflict. They wanted to do a grab bag in the same way

---

2   Rock, *The House Without a Christmas Tree.*

the kids in this 1946 story did, by picking names. The boy who had drawn Evan's name wasn't going to be in class the day of the party, so he brought in Evan's grab-bag gift the day before. Evan saw no reason for waiting to open it. Thus, the day before the party, he was demanding nonstop that he be given his gift.

Around Passover, we would read about the customs of a Jewish immigrant family and their loving relationships in the novel *All-of-a-Kind Family.*[3] Elementary students refer to these novels as "chapter books." They should be on every fifth-grader's reading list. So should *Hatchet,*[4] a story about adventure, survival, and the emotional upheaval caused by divorce. My students read along in *Hatchet* while listening to the fabulous audiotape narrated by Peter Coyote—what a voice! It was the only book we read this way, and the kids loved it. In fact, each year my students requested that new chapters not be played unless there was 100 percent attendance in the room.

R.I.P. —THE EGG TOSS

Administrators in my school district took a dim view of the egg-toss contest, even though I had

3   Taylor, *All-of-a-Kind Family.*
4   Paulsen, *Hatchet.*

been doing it with great relish and success—and without a mishap—for umpteen years before they found out about it. Evidently, they never attended an American Legion or a Veterans of Foreign Wars family picnic, where all the kids and some of the adults enjoyed participating in such mayhem. Three-legged races and oranges being passed under the chin from one person to another were all part of the fun at these picnics, which I attended as a youth. The orange game was especially popular with the adults; so was lining up across from a partner who, after a successful underhanded first toss of a raw egg, stepped backward, as did each subsequent tosser, creating an ever-increasing distance that eventually caused most eggs to drop and break on the ground.

I was eventually told that this "unsafe and dangerous" activity would have to cease because a child could be "maimed for life." Thus, I had to cancel the egg toss for Evan's class. (I wonder, though, just how many lawsuits are brought against our military-service organizations each year for the personal injuries caused by this and other "harmful and dangerous" activities at their family picnics. Has anyone been "maimed for life" or even bruised?)

Many of the children in my class were siblings of former students, so their parents were familiar with the games played at our Halloween party. Needless to say, they were dismayed when I had to cancel this activity. (That is, all except for one mother. She feared her son could get salmonella poisoning as a result of touching and tossing a raw egg. Evidently, unlike Evan and his classmates, she hadn't been taught about the miraculous power of hand-washing in preventing the spread of this and other diseases.)

My darling ten-year-olds would just have to set aside their egging compulsions until they went trick-or-treating after school in their neighborhoods.

Can you imagine the furor that would have resulted if a school administrator had discovered the shaving-cream battles that were part of my Halloween repertoire when I was a younger teacher?

CHAPTER 4

Gearing Up for Melting Down

SET-UP FOR STRESS

Days off were hard on Evan.

I'd been reading *A Parent's Guide to Asperger Syndrome and High-Functioning Autism.*[5] Evan's dad had given me this insightful book. I recommend it highly. Its authors indicate that kids with Asperger syndrome need a consistent routine and schedule. Good advice!

---

5   Ozonoff, Dawson, and McPartland. *A Parent's Guide to Asperger Syndrome and High-Functioning Autism.*

But in public schools, about the only thing you can count on is change. No two days are ever alike. And the month of November is especially broken up with days off due to Election Day, Veterans Day, Thanksgiving, parent/teacher conferences, and teacher training for things like The JASON Project. Certainly, this is not an optimal environment for an autistic child.

The New York State Social Studies Test was also scheduled for the third week of November. This test was basically a rigorous Regent's exam and covered history, geography, economics, social issues, and civics, from the dawn of man to present day. Multiple-choice questions and a section on constructed responses were scheduled for the first day, and an essay question based on original historical documents for the next. If you took the stress created by this test and coupled it with all the changes in routine, you had a perfect formula for a meltdown—anybody's meltdown.

TEACHERS' STRESS

The pressure on teachers was tremendous.

Students needed to review everything they previously learned (or were supposed to have learned and remembered) in social studies since third grade. They also had to learn how to write a creditable essay predicated on old pictures, charts, graphs, newspaper accounts, and other historical, archival documents.

When I mentioned that questions could be based on patriotic songs, one of my students actually said, "Oh, like, 'Jose, can you see'?" Although comedians use this line as a joke, this ten-year-old really thought that was the name of our national anthem.

I recall a test question about the effect that the low bridges had on passengers' behavior in a song about the Erie Canal. Fortunately, fifth-grade teachers had asked the vocal-music teacher to go over this "popular ditty" and similar songs before the test.

Another student identified a pen-and-ink drawing of a snowshoe as an Indian tennis racket—not a totally unexpected answer from a kid who lived south of Fordham Road in New York's urbanized suburbia. The following year, we sought help from our physical-education teachers.

EVAN'S STRESS

When Evan arrived in class on November 18, the day before the dreaded test, he announced in a piercing voice that he needed the top of one of his two desks cleaned off. There was no room to put down his stuff. This was the second time he had requested such help. Although I accommodated him, I wouldn't have dreamt of doing so for another fifth-grader—or for a third-grader, or for any regular-education student for that matter. I left the daily agenda partially completed on the board and hurriedly opened the blinds and windows before going to his desk. (Once I got involved with Evan, there was no telling when I would get back to carrying out normal routines.)

As I moved his things onto an adjacent desk, he kept grabbing his pencils and other items back. I had to tell him that I was just putting his things there temporarily. We then discussed what he wanted to keep and what could be discarded. He was concerned that some of his DBQs (document-based essay questions) and practice-test packets seemed to be missing. (They were supposed to have gone home.) He was relieved to learn that I had already retrieved them from the mess and put them on his chair. He seemed to be watching me, but was he really seeing what I was doing?

Among the packets was Part 1 of the multiple-choice questions from an old test. He hadn't made an answer sheet, but he had circled the answers on the reproduced test booklet. I asked his classmate Jarred, who had scored 100 percent on this section, to take his own answer sheet and mark Evan's test. As Evan considered himself to be on the same academic level as Jarred, he wasn't the least bit upset when I asked Jarred to do this.

Thirteen wrong! That meant that Evan only scored 63 percent. Prior to this, he had completed two multiple-choice practice tests and scored in the 80s on both. I was stunned and began stammering, "Thirteen wrong! Thirteen wrong. My brilliant student got thirteen wrong?" This got his attention and he said, "Can I do it over?" I replied, "Not if you're going to get another 63."

I gave him another copy of the test, but he just put it on his desk and went to find *Newsday* so he could work on the crossword puzzle. He was about to become annoyed because the students' papers hadn't been delivered to our classroom, but it didn't become an issue because I flipped him my copy. As the morning progressed, he came up to the table, which elongates my desk, with one of his favorite crossword books. He enjoyed sitting in the big, ugly, orange, vinyl desk chair stationed at this table. (I had purchased this rolling chair at a garage sale for about three dollars. This is the standard way teachers furnish their classrooms.) He knew that I saw he wasn't doing his assigned morning work, but neither of us mentioned it.

DEALING

As we worked, we chatted.

"Are you going to let me down tomorrow by getting another 63?"

Evan just shrugged his shoulders.

"What could I do to make you interested enough to get a higher score?"

After contemplating this for a moment, he said, "Some extra time in the computer lab—there's a website I want to try out."

I reminded him that due to the way the school computers were censored, he might not be able to get to that site. He said he thought that he'd be able to get to it—he loved outwitting the censors. I agreed to arrange for additional time in the computer lab if he would retake the practice test and improve his score. He wanted to know by how much. "Would, like, an 83 do it?" he asked.

I said that anything above an 80 percent would be fine.

I then wrote a note to the resource-room teacher asking if Evan could work independently on a retest in her room. Sure enough, he came back from there with a test paper that had only five wrong answers. I wondered—if I had said that I would only settle for a grade of 90 or better, would I have gotten that?

THE HAZARDS OF TESTING

On November 19, the first day of the test, Evan arrived bopping up and down and twirling while wandering around the classroom. I hadn't prepared him individually for the fact that we would be taking Part 1 of the real New York State Social Studies Test first and that everything else on the daily schedule would be moved around. I incorrectly assumed that he would have remembered the testing routine from the fourth grade, so I guess I deserved what happened next.

Ready, Set, Oh No!
First, the children had to move their desks from groups into straight rows with appropriate spacing in between. When I noticed that Evan wasn't

moving his desk, I suggested to Anna that she should move up her desk, thus allowing Evan to just turn his desk. Instead, she moved his desk for him. Her touching his desk really irritated him, and he let her and everyone else know it by screaming that she was messing with his stuff. It was the beginning of the end.

As I began passing out the test booklets, I noticed that Evan's desktop was once again in a state of chaos.

"Would you like me to help you straighten your desktop?" I asked.

"No, no, no-o-o-o-o."

Evan then began groaning and flailing around in his seat.

"You know you are going to have to settle down or you won't be able to take your test in here."

Ignoring History

Actually, I hadn't wanted Evan to take his test in our classroom. His fourth-grade teacher warned me that he'd had a meltdown the prior year while taking the state math test and had to be removed from the classroom. I brought this fact up at a Child Study Team meeting. My goal in seeking an alternative testing site was not only to help Evan but also to provide my other students with a quiet testing period. If Evan had been classified as a student in need of special-education services, most likely a provision would have been put into his IEP (Individualized Education Plan) for such a testing venue. But Evan had no IEP.

Thus, I was amazed when the principal said that she would allow Evan to take the test in a different setting. It was suggested that Evan could take the test either with the inclusion students or in the resource room. As the special-education inclusion students would be read the questions aloud, the quieter resource room seemed a better choice. Evan was more than capable of reading the test questions and had recently taken the retest there.

For some reason not communicated to me, this plan was changed at the last minute on the morning of the test. Evan was now scheduled to take the test in our classroom. If an IEP had been in place, I am almost positive that Evan would have been given the test in an appropriate setting, no matter what.

Melting Down

Evan became increasingly agitated as I read the directions for the test. He began to bellow and chant, "I want attention. I want attention." I stopped reading and waited for him to quiet down. A few of Evan's classmates tried to cajole him into behaving appropriately, but this only made the situation worse. Evan then began ranting and railing against everything.

Perhaps it was past the time for "let's make a deal," but I didn't know what else to do. So, I walked over to Evan's desk and said, "You can take the test here and earn time in the computer lab, or you can work on it out in the hall or maybe in the resource room." (Of course, I was bluffing about the last two options.)

Just then, the resource-room teacher came into our room. Another of my special-needs students, who had left to take her test there, had told Mrs. J. that Evan was out of control. When Evan saw this teacher, he lost it. He became hysterical and began shrieking. As I didn't have any choice, I ignored him and pretended to chat amicably with Mrs. J. This took all our acting skills.

What should we do? How can we remove him physically from the room? Who can we call to help?

No policy was in place to cover such a situation, even though the same thing had happened in fourth grade. I certainly wondered as to the identity of the "genius" who changed his test setting back to the classroom.

I recalled reading somewhere that when a child like Evan was in meltdown, he wanted to be in a safe environment, near someone he trusted. Evan wanted "Mama," and right now, I was "Mama."

Maybe Evan realized this too, for he suddenly stopped and began to settle down. I asked the resource-room teacher to leave but to send her aide back to me in about ten minutes to check on how things were going. As I left Evan's desk, I bent down and reminded him that the computer-lab time was based on his passing the test with a score of 80 percent or better, just like I had required yesterday. He said nothing in response but continued groaning and then humming as he worked. Fortunately, my other students said nothing about all the noise. I am sure that his antics were extremely distracting.

Sneaky Tactics
Evan finished the multiple-choice section quickly, which presented another problem. I needed to

visually scan his test to see if indeed he had scored at least 80 percent. That meant I had to make a master list of answers immediately, while proctoring the test and being available to other students who might need another pencil, etc. Luckily, Evan decided to sit in the orange chair and work, though not silently, on the *Newsday* crossword puzzle. It didn't seem to bother him that the top of my table was covered with all sorts of testing paraphernalia. I was able to work out the answers and saw that he had most of them correct. He had legitimately earned time in the computer lab, which would get him and his noises out of the room. I also noticed that he had not finished the Constructed Response Section of the exam. This section contained items such as illustrations, charts, and graphs, followed by questions based on them. As he was preparing to leave, I quietly asked him when he thought he'd get to this section, and he replied in an affected stage whisper, "After snack time."

Evan and I both knew that this was a timed test, that he wasn't finished, and that snack time would follow only after the test's completion. However, I wasn't about to cause another meltdown by preventing him from leaving the room. I also knew that I was completely on my own. The resource-room aide never came to check on how things were progressing, and a call for help that I had made earlier to the main office had been fielded by the school secretary. She said she would have the principal get back to me.

I was also pretty sure that I couldn't give him extended time to finish the test without an IEP being in place. In any event, Evan returned quickly from the computer lab, stating the network wasn't available. Now he wanted to try the computer in our classroom, which I told him would have the same problem. He wanted to try it anyway and assured me he'd turn down the sound. I said the sound was to be off. He thought about arguing with me, but didn't. At this point, I would have given in to him on just about anything.

Evan discovered that the class computer was no better, so he brought one of his crossword books (from his limitless supply) to the front table, where he worked once again on top of all the papers. I waited until he seemed calmer before I retrieved his test booklet and put the last page of the Constructed Response Section under his nose. I pointed out that there were only two "itsy-bitsy" questions requiring answers. These questions were based on preceding information in the booklet, but I didn't mention that. Evan growled at me but filled in the answers without even glancing at the relevant information. I then turned to another page and pointed to where answers were required. Working backwards in this manner, he answered all the questions in the Constructed Response Section. I glanced at the clock and saw that he had done so within the allotted time. In fact, all my students completed the test within the established time.

I was exhausted, but that feeling soon changed to exhilaration when I unofficially marked those two sections of Evan's test and found that he had scored an eighty-nine on the multiple-choice section and a perfect fourteen points on the Constructed Response Section. All of my other students passed both sections of the test, too.

My students had been instructed to record all their answers on scrap paper so that I could quickly check and grade them. I based my "unofficial grade" of the multiple-choice answers on one hundred points, and I kept the information of the results of both sections of the test on a separate tally sheet. That way, there was no room for shenanigans when others officially handled and marked the tests. It also gave me instant information about what my students knew and what I still needed to teach.

The children who were nearest to where Evan was carrying on did about the same as they had done on practice tests, but had it been peaceful and quiet, would they have been able to achieve even higher scores? I suspected that might be true, but I couldn't say for sure because that afternoon no one complained to me, and they usually did when Evan's antics annoyed them.

Drama Queen

Part 2 of the test, the Document-Based Essay Question, was to be administered the next day—November 20. Evan was scheduled to take this section of the test in the computer lab, but not using the computer. I tried to prepare him for this by having the special-education inclusion teacher walk him through the actual procedures he would be expected to follow. I didn't want to chance another meltdown—my other kids deserved better.

I also didn't want another change of venue. I had made this perfectly clear to those in charge by hyperventilating in the faculty room at lunchtime on that first day of testing.

My dramatic rendition of what had happened that morning worked better for getting what I wanted than going into the principal's office and begging for help. (I had learned this effective theatrical strategy early on in my career.) Interestingly, there wasn't an administrator present at the time of my performance.

So, Evan would definitely be taking Part 2 of the test elsewhere.

The Second Day of Testing

Once again, Evan arrived at school bopping and twirling. He began singing and howling as I tried to organize the class for this part of the test. I was almost finished with reading the test directions when a person—different than the one Evan and I expected—arrived to escort Evan and his test booklet to the lab. Would she, not the regular computer-lab teaching assistant, be supervising Evan's exam? Was it any wonder why both Evan and I got so frustrated and confused?

A Placid DBQ

There would certainly be more confusion to come, but for a while, during the DBQ section of the test, peace and quiet reigned. The regular computer-lab teaching assistant informed me that Evan had worked quickly to complete the comprehension questions and his essay. He wanted to return to our classroom as soon as he was done. However, she kept him there for the entire period. This proved beneficial, as that morning I had questioned several students about Evan's conduct during Part 1 of the test. They felt that his outrageous behavior had interfered with their concentration, and some feared that it might have negatively affected their scores. (I allayed their fears by letting them know that they had all, by my figuring, passed Part 1.)

The calm that permeated the classroom during the test on day two enabled all my students to write well-thought-out essays. In fact, when scores from all the sections were "officially" combined several weeks later at the conclusion of the massive district-wide scoring rally (which I never attended following the first disconcerting one), most of my students (seventeen out of twenty-five) earned 4s—the highest grade—including Evan.

(Note: This particular test was dropped after I had Evan. Many other tests dealing with reading and math skills but not social studies were added.)

CHAPTER 5

ABA Standoff

A RUSSIAN STRATEGY?

One method touted for teaching children with autism is called "ABA." According to a guru brought in by our district's Special Education Department for a parents' meeting on the evening of January 7, it is the only method that works.

As the presenter explained it, the "A" is something that the child wants. The "B" is something the teacher or parent wants the child to do. If the child does the "B," he gets the "A." This presenter insisted that ABA must be done 100 percent of the time. He urged parents to be unrelenting in using it.

Ivan Pavlov studied and wrote about external conditioned reflex and learning in the late nineteenth and early twentieth centuries, so this psychological phenomenon struck me as not exactly a new, groundbreaking behavior-modification strategy. A special-education teacher in my school district later told me that ABA stands for "applied behavior analysis." It's based on the work of behavioral psychologist Ivar Lovaas, who pioneered the development of specific ABA techniques for use with autistic children.

When I inquired about what other teachers were doing, a special-education teacher in another district said she used strategies based on a B. F. Skinner's "antecedents-behavior-consequences" operant-conditioning model. This approach examines the triggers or antecedents that cause negative behavior and teaches appropriate responses.

The authors of *A Parent's Guide to Asperger Syndrome and High-Functioning Autism* refer to treatment programs such as TEACCH (Treatment and Education of Autistic and related Communication-handicapped CHildren) developed by Eric Schopler; the Denver Treatment Model developed by Sally Rogers; and the Greenspan Model, developed by Stanley Greenspan. There are probably other behavior-modification approaches, too. The anointed guru, however, didn't impart any of this information and gave the impression that the ABA method, as he presented it, was the one and only model.

ABA was something that I tried with Evan. "Deal-making" was my version of this strategy, and I think Evan used it more on me than vice versa. But did ABA always work? What was changed because of using it? And was it worth the struggle?

SIX HOURS OF ABA

Here is how a six-hour day of trying to stick to *my version* of ABA went on Tuesday, January 20.

Evan is not doing his assigned work. Instead, he is fooling around with a magnifying glass. I turn off the class computer, which is something Evan looks forward to using. It is used as the "A" for getting him to do the "B." He notices what I do, but is not at all upset because he is concentrating on the magnifying glass. He also can tell by glancing at the daily agenda, which is always printed on the board, that later in the morning our class will be going as a group to the computer lab, and he will be able to go online. Thus, he will be getting the "A" later without doing the "B" now. I should have taken the magnifying glass away and then given it back when his assignment was completed, but that couldn't have been done without a physical struggle—a definite "no-no" in public schools.

Later, in the computer lab, Evan is doing his own thing. The class assignment is to work on "A Walk through the Canopy," one of the computer labs that is part of this year's JASON Project science curriculum.

Evan insists that he already did this lab at home, although he says he didn't save it. He adds that he has completed all the labs. I have no reason to doubt him, as he usually relishes doing computer assignments. So now he feels justified in doing his own thing, in spite of the fact that I modify his assignment by telling him to work on the "Race to Reforest" lab, this time by changing a variable.

I disengage. (Evan growls.)

In the black-and-white world of autism, I believe that Evan rationalizes that he has already com-pleted the assignment as expressly stated and feels vindicated in not complying with the change in a directive aimed specifically at him. I realize this when he doesn't try for a deal of his own.

I am thoroughly frustrated. I feel like growling too. The computers in the lab are all turned on and there is no other place to send Evan. I could turn off his computer, but knowing Evan, he'd launch into a tirade, and no one else would be able to work. In fact, his ranting could go on for the rest of the day, and as the day progresses, that's exactly what happens.

There is also nothing else that he wants that can be used for the "A," except that he doesn't want me to call his father. In my teacher's world, noncompliance with assignments is an ongoing, common challenge. I feel that I need to save the "I'm going to call Dad unless you do…" for more important confrontations. As things developed, I couldn't have been more wrong. But during the computer lab, once again, Evan gets the "A" without doing the "B."

NO MAGIC BULLET

In retrospect, I should have known better than to pick the day after our Martin Luther King Jr.

holiday for trying to stick to any form of ABA. A day off from established school routine (even a day that elongates a weekend) plus our opposing positions on the labs, coupled with my rashness in sticking to ABA, resulted in the following sequence of events:

During the indoor lunch/recess period, Evan gives the adult lunchroom monitor a hard time. He wants the classroom computer turned on. (So now he wants the "A.") I had told the monitor before I went to lunch that the computer was to remain off and that she wasn't to give in to him.

Evan decides to bolt from the room. He is intercepted in the hall by the resource-room teacher, Mrs. J., who just happened to be walking by. After listening to his litany of complaints, she assures Evan that she'll talk to me about restoring his computer privileges. Mrs. J. catches me in the faculty lunchroom, but I am relentless. "No computer until he does…."

When I return to the classroom, Evan is sitting in front of the lifeless computer, waiting for me. I get his agenda book and work folder, ignoring him. While sitting at my desk, I remove his homework and put marked and corrected work into his folder. As I write in his agenda book, Evan comes up to my desk to see what I am writing, but decides instead to play with my stapler. Along with his daily work, I write down his homework assignments and the date for the makeup test on the state capitals, which he failed. I add that fact in the note to his dad and ask him to call me that evening at home. When Evan finally notices what I wrote, he goes ballistic. He grabs the book and scribbles out the retest info. He then gets into my desk drawer where I keep, among other things, a hammer that I used to use to open old classroom windows. Evan begins swinging the hammer over my head. J. T. yells, "Watch out, he'll hit you!" As I duck, I reply—with more aplomb than I feel—"That will be the day!"

Just then, Mrs. P., the computer-teaching assistant, comes in and notices the chaos. Her presence helps subdue Evan's outburst a bit, and while he is distracted I grab the hammer. Still, he is very agitated and takes his agenda book and slams it on the floor, screaming, "I hate my life! Call my mother, I want to kill myself!" With that said, he takes a metal spoon from the same drawer and, holding it like it was a knife, pretends to stab himself and falls to the floor.

Knowing I have to change his focus and get his mind off himself, I tell him the Irish could have done the temper tantrum better—though I doubt it. One of my students, Katie, and I improvise a real, red-headed Irish temper tantrum. This seems to get everyone giggling, including Evan, and it dissipates a lot of the tension in the room. Mrs. P. now feels free to leave. However, I notice that Charles is visibly upset with what just transpired. "Is he really going to kill himself?" he asks.

Now it's time for a "face-off." This peer-mediation technique requires students to face each other while each one takes a turn telling the other what they think happened and why they are angry or upset. While one student is talking, the other one may only listen.

I take both boys out in the hall. While facing each other almost nose-to-nose, Charles explains to Evan how scared he felt when Evan said he wanted to kill himself. I urge Evan to allay Charles's fear by telling him he wasn't serious—just a drama queen.

(Note: Although I never viewed Evan as suicidal while he was in my class, researchers report that there is a high incidence of suicide for adults with this syndrome. They believe depression caused by isolation may be the causal factor.)

Upon reentering the room, I tell Evan that I want him to sit in the orange chair and help me check off completed work packets. Helping the teacher has the desired calming effect. Now looking for some sympathy, Evan says, "Just put down Fs for me."

Later, Evan, without being prompted, brings his agenda book back up to me so that I can rerecord what he scribbled out. He still has not done any of his assignments, but the day closes on a calmer note. (I wish I could say that Charles and I felt calmer.)

Most of the time today, Evan didn't need to do the "B" to get the "A." Other times, he vacillated between wanting and not wanting the "A." He certainly could manipulate situations better than I could. Was the upheaval caused by my trying to stick to ABA worth it?

POSTSCRIPT

After school, the music teacher dropped by to tell me that Evan's dad hadn't returned her most recent phone call. I replied, "We only have Evan for six hours; his parents have him the rest." She responded, "Some days even a forty-two-minute period seems too long."

CHAPTER 6

Advice from Umpires

CREATE WIN-WIN SITUATIONS

Articles written by scholars about Asperger syndrome urge teachers not to let classmates pick teams or groups, as their research shows that the Asperger child gets left for last. This is good advice for rookie teachers, designated hitters, and seasoned veterans because "being picked last" happens to other children too. So, as the "club's manager," a teacher should oversee the makeup of cooperative groups and establish the lineup of all teams. Also, an all-girls team and all-boys team should never be pitted against each other.

When a former third-grade student of mine was placed in my classroom to do a series of observations for her college class, I encouraged her to teach a few mini-lessons. On her last day, she presented a *Jeopardy!*-type activity and set up teams of mixed abilities and gender. Evan's broad spectrum of knowledge helped his team score many points and win the game.

In science, Evan's keen interest in observing and experimenting with crayfish led me to pick him to be a leader of one of the group investigation teams. There were a few complaints about Evan's hogging the crayfish, but not enough for me to consider replacing him.

"YADA, YADA, YADA!"

"Quiet" and "calm" are attributes mentioned in articles discussing the best learning environment for children with ASD (autism spectrum disorders). School administrators should keep this advice in mind when they place students.

This redhead and her students were anything but calm and quiet. Being of Irish decent, I believe in the adage that "you are a long time dead" and a classroom that is quiet seems dead to me. I like a classroom where there is a great deal of inter-action. When I saw that a student may not have understood something that I had just taught—no matter how brilliantly executed the lesson was—I would often ask another student to explain it again to that individual. (Thus, even when my students were doing what is called "busy work" during skills-practice periods, it was noisy.)

Evan occasionally functioned as this kind of peer tutor, although he'd make it clear that he was doing so only as a favor to me and that he would expect something in return. Such requests on my part were greeted with lots of groaning on his part, but I continued to make them in order to keep him involved with his classmates.

HITS AND ERRORS

Did my noisy, casual classroom and multisensory, interdisciplinary approach create an overwhelming environment that triggered some of Evan's socially abusive behaviors? Maybe so. Then again, when Evan decided to twirl around the room or twiddle with an innocuous object or gripe and grumble, he didn't stick out as much as he would have in a classroom where physical movement and vocal chatter were curtailed.

But Evan wasn't always engaged in mayhem. Occasionally, I would notice him engrossed in a serious conversation with a peer, and when he was, it made my day.

CHAPTER 7

Coffee and the Spelling Bee

COFFEE = COOPERATION

I didn't realize that Evan had drunk coffee in the morning before he came to school; nor did I remember that it was the day of the final round of the fifth-grade spelling bee. Instead, I was preoccupied with Evan's raspy voice.

Evan had a cold and sore throat and, based on prior experience with his colds, I knew he'd be sharing his with me. New York teachers always know from whom they catch their colds, and Evan had given me a few beauties already.

Although I was used to his hanging on me, when he was feeling sick he never left my side. If I was sitting, he'd put his head on my shoulder; if I was standing, his skin was touching my skin.

I decided to send him to the nurse, even though I knew the chances of his being sent home were slim to none. The fact that three of my students were out with strep throat wouldn't influence her decision unless he had a temperature. So, maybe I sent him to the nurse's office just to get a brief respite from his hanging. I was scheduled to attend a conference at the United Nations the next day, and I didn't want to miss it because I was sick. As expected, he soon returned to our classroom, stating that he didn't have a temperature.

Perhaps my preoccupation with the upcoming conference was why I missed the fact that Evan had had coffee at Dunkin' Donuts that morning with his mom. It hadn't even registered when he was telling me about buying his love, Valarie, a doughnut with pink icing and sprinkles. (Since Evan talked nonstop, I often listened with only half an ear.)

Coffee seemed to positively affect Evan's behavior; so, as sick as he was, he was very cooperative. He had promised me that he would try to complete a math makeup test on harder multiplication examples and problems if I didn't write a note to his dad about his first failed attempt, and he intended to keep his promise. Thus, the early morning was calm (even though Evan was unable to solve most of the problems). He complained a few times that I wasn't guiding him through the examples like his father did when they worked on them at home. I told him that this was a test and to get on with it, but I privately lamented for the thousandth time that if Evan had an aide, guiding him through the exam would have been possible. Later, when I was hobbling down the corridor, following my students on the way to the computer lab, Evan stayed back and tried to help me. (I was walking with great difficulty because I needed orthopedic surgery, and I was now using a cane.) Evan's courtly action toward me reminded me of a nineteenth-century gentleman.

SPRINKLES SPELL "L - O - V - E"

It wasn't until snack time that I glanced over at Valarie's desk and noticed the paper bag from Dunkin' Donuts, on top of which was a doughnut with pink icing and sprinkles. (I suspected that Evan's mom was advising him about appropriate romantic overtures.) A doughnut for Valarie meant coffee for Evan. Now I knew why he was being so cooperative; but more important, this also meant that Evan would be totally focused on the spelling bee in the afternoon. He was one of the two finalists representing our class and, if Evan was focused, I knew he would win.

WAY TO GO!

When he did win, my class went wild with applause, and there were lots of high-fives as Evan returned to where we were sitting. There had also been some very loud hooting when he won, which I discovered was coming from me. A PTA representative presented him and the runner-up with prizes that, even wrapped, looked suspiciously like dictionaries. Giving a kid who can spell a dictionary didn't seem like an appropriate prize to me, a nonspeller, and I wasn't sure how Evan would react when he opened it. He sat practically on my lap while he ripped the paper off. I leaned over and, speaking in a disappointed tone of voice that only he could hear, said, "Oh no, a dictionary." With that said, Evan turned to me while hugging the new dictionary to his chest and replied, "But I love dictionaries."

CHAPTER 8

About Being "Terrific"

MANDATED ASSEMBLY PROGRAM

Being a perfectionist, Evan wanted to redo the paper mat that he had been weaving in art class. The art teacher refused to let anyone do so. Thus, when I returned to the classroom after my prep period, I found him in a snit. He wanted material to make a better mat, and he wanted it immediately. I told him that I'd give him, and anyone else who wanted it, some paper when we returned from the "mandated" Terrific Kids assembly. He began to argue that this wasn't acceptable. He was sure that I wouldn't give him the supplies, just like the art teacher who had refused him. Therefore, I showed him where the colored paper was stored in my cupboard and left him alone in the classroom. He would have to choose what he would do.

Evan appeared in the all-purpose room a few minutes later and joined me where I was sitting with his classmates. I whispered to him that he had no faith in me, and that I always tried to do what I said I would do. He quietly apologized and said that he not only lacked faith in me—he also lacked faith in himself. This assembly was indeed hard to sit through if you're not being recognized as "terrific," and half way through it Evan asked if he could go back to the classroom and work on the art project. I responded that I had faith in him; therefore, he could go back to the classroom. Allowing a student to work alone in a classroom is another definite "no-no" in public schools. However, I needed to make my point with Evan, and I knew I could trust him.

SOME TERRIFIC; MOST NOT

I found this assembly program even harder to sit through than Evan did. The way the Kiwanis "Terrific Kids" program was implemented in my school building enabled only one student a month per fifth-grade class to be recognized as "terrific." So, from the get-go, approximately fifteen students per class were not going to be deemed "terrific" during the course of the year. They would not get to bask in the applause of their classmates. They would not get to shake hands with the representatives of this *fine* community-service organization. They would not receive a bumper sticker for their parent's car with the Kiwanis logo, which again proclaimed them as "terrific."

In September, two student representatives from each fifth-grade class met to establish criteria for this award. Year after year, the list of attributes the students developed consisted of many of the same adjectives that described the behaviors of Girl or Boy Scouts. Then, each month, students nominated a classmate for this honor by writing that person's name on a large paper ballot. They also had to include their reasons for selecting this person, based on the established criteria. The student receiving the most nominations or votes won. To adults this may sound rational and fair, but with fifth-graders, after the first month or so, it became a popularity contest. I hated picking up the pieces back in the classroom following this assembly, when disappointed ten-year-olds wondered aloud why they weren't chosen.

ARGUING MY POINT

I've tried writing letters to administrators, arguing with my colleagues, and talking to members of the sponsoring organization in order to either change the number of eligible students or eradicate my class's participation. Members of the Kiwanis told me that they leave it up to the individual school to determine the criteria for the Terrific Kids Award and the number of students eligible.

Can you imagine a ten-year-old who is not terrific at something? I can't. I think it's a teacher's job to catch students being terrific or to teach them how to be terrific. So every year I attempted to manipulate the program by having ties or picking additional students myself, based on the reason(s) cited by their classmates. By doing this, I tried to ensure that each of my students was deemed "terrific" for something. (I didn't always succeed, as the principal seemed to be on to me.)

Evan was accorded this distinction early in the year. He was selected because a girl in my class wrote that, along with his meeting a few of the criteria, she felt he "needed this kind of recognition." Can you imagine if *she* wasn't selected as "terrific"?

CHAPTER 9

Fail the Kid

REWARDING FAILURE

There's a song in the play *Guys and Dolls* that urges a woman to "marry the man today and change his ways tomorrow." Change these words slightly to "fail the kid today and reap the rewards tomorrow" and you'll have the "solution" I found for getting some help for my Asperger student.

Until I gave Evan a failing report-card grade in math, nobody on the school's Child Study Team held out any hope for my getting additional assistance for dealing with all his special needs. Maybe the fact that I told members of the team that I was planning to go before the board of education with this problem helped too. I explained (with tongue in cheek) that I wasn't planning to politely ask board members for help while standing respectfully at the podium. I told the committee that I would role-play a student with outrageous behaviors at the board's next monthly meeting.

"What's the worst thing they could do to me?" I asked. "Have me arrested?"

If anyone knows the history of board of education meetings in my district, calling the police and having irate citizens threatened with arrest was—how shall I put this—not unheard of. But the members of the Child Study Team were unaware of this history and the fact that, in this instance, I was bluffing.

6 X 4 ≠ JACKIE ROBINSON; 6 X 7 DOES

Evan failed math because he had been unable to pass even abridged forms of the end-of-chapter tests that I had inflicted upon my students during the second marking period. He also had been unable to demonstrate mastery of harder multiplication facts or an understanding of underlying multiplication concepts. (Yes, Evan had failed the state-capitals tests, but those two tests didn't impact his social studies grade the same way that the math tests affected his math grade.)

I explained all this to his parents in a supplementary progress report, which I had sent to them by snail mail a week or two earlier. However, they must not have mentioned anything about it to Evan. Since I conference with each child about his or her report card several days before it is taken home, Evan asked me what the NP stood for under math. I explained that it meant "not passing." Upon hearing this, Evan's eyes almost popped out of their sockets. I quickly followed my explanation of his grade with the fact that his parents were already aware of it. This seemed to astonish him even more than the failing grade.

"My father knows?" he asked.

"Yes, he has known for a while, and he's probably not upset with you because he knows you've been trying." I could see disbelief register on Evan's face as he walked away from my desk, utterly astounded.

But Evan wasn't the only one to be surprised for the next day during lunch in the faculty room, the school psychologist showed me a draft of a document she had entitled "Principal's Intervention Plan."

Heretofore, the existence of such an intervention plan was known to those in special-education circles and referred to in my school district as a "PIP," but its existence was virtually unknown to me, a thirty-seven-year "regular-education" teacher.

Earlier, I had sent the psychologist a note regarding Evan's failed math tests during the second marking period and added that this was disgraceful for a boy with an IQ as high as his. (Since I treated the state-capitals tests as anomalies, I prudently ignored them in my note to her, as overkill can backfire.)

Evidently, his failing grade was the straw that got the camel moving. The psychologist wanted to know if I would look over the PIP and see if it met Evan's most pressing needs. Was there anything that I thought should be added? I, like Evan, was stunned.

A LONG HAUL

In the past, members of the Child Study Team had told me on two separate occasions that because Evan was such a high-functioning student, he didn't qualify for a special-education designation or services. Both his parents and I had requested such a designation, as we recognized that we were doing things with Evan the hard way. The fact that he became so frustrated and anxious during high-stakes testing situations, which caused him to howl and chant as he had in the fall during the state test, had been, in the committee's opinion, "just unfortunate."

Yes, unfortunate for my other twenty-four students who had to complete the timed test with all that distraction going on. His behavior, in the opinion of the Child Study Team members, hadn't been reason enough for a "504 Plan" to be established, either. Minutes before this meeting, I had been told by a special-education teacher (on the sly) that a 504 Plan might provide me with additional help for Evan. However, I knew nothing else about a 504 and the novice teacher who alluded to it was afraid to tell me more. Nothing had ever been mentioned to me about a PIP, either.

Why all the secrecy? Money? Of course, if I had known more about what was available for a student like Evan with special needs, I'd have gone towards it like a charging bull. What tenured teacher in the same circumstances wouldn't?

The fact that Evan had the same problems in fourth grade hadn't strengthened my argument with the Child Study Team. Even Evan's outrageous, well-documented behaviors had had no bearing on the situation. But now, because of a failing report-card grade in math, a PIP would be put in place. I read it, savoring every word.

The plan allowed Evan the following concessions:

~ To use the computer lab and utilize the computer when he needs a break from class

~ To bring his work to the resource room if he needs a quieter setting in which to work

~ To receive assistance from the resource-room teacher or teacher's aide for five to ten minutes at the beginning of the day to help him organize his work and get started

~ To get assistance from the resource-room teacher or aide in packing up his work at the end of the day

~ To receive modified classroom tests, such as in limiting the number of questions that he is required to complete and extra time to complete tests

~ To be tested in a separate location in order to minimize distractions

This plan amounted to so little, but did help, even though the services it provided for weren't always forthcoming or available; nor did it specifically address his failure in math. In fact, I had already started doing some of these things on my own without "official" sanction.

What Evan really needed was a full-time aide, but that was not to be.

CHAPTER 10

Hurdles

SELF-PERCEPTION

I was talking to a substitute teacher whom I hadn't seen in a long time when Evan wedged his way in between us. In a very formal manner I introduced Evan to her. Evan responded to her nod of recognition by saying, "Yeah, I'm an interesting specimen." I wanted to respond by saying, "Aren't we all!" but the opportunity passed too quickly. I promised myself that I would get back to Evan about his self-perception the next time we had an up-close-and-personal conversation.

Such conversations usually took place after I calmed him down from some perceived or real injustice or stopped him from carrying on a repetitive behavior like Windexing[6] everything and everyone in the classroom. He was usually quite contrite and full of promises of amendment, so it was a good time to talk.

FATHER KNOWS BEST

One of our face-to-face conversations dealt with the fact that if it wasn't for his father's persistence in getting him to do almost everything expected, he wouldn't be the capable student that he was.

Deep down, Evan knew this to be true, but that didn't stop him from trying to keep as much information as possible from Dad. Reports sent home about his lack of progress on pencil-and-paper assignments or tasks requiring memorization were trigger points that caused much consternation.

---

6   OSHA take note: students used my old Windex spray bottles, which were emptied, rinsed, and refilled with plain or soapy water, to clean their desktops, etc.

HANDWRITING ASSIGNMENTS

I'd read that children with Asperger syndrome often experience difficulty with printing and hand-writing skills, and Evan was no exception.

Negotiating away his daily handwriting assignment was his first priority. When his newly acquired aide, Mrs. Lillis, copied the daily handwriting assignment into his agenda book under the heading of things that he should complete in school, it caused hysterics. Evan knew that his father would make him complete this assignment at home if he left it undone in school, and he wanted no part of it.

I also noticed that Evan had trouble with other fine motor skills too. Retrieving books from inside his desk, getting items out of folders, and turning pages all seemed to present some difficulty. I asked the school psychologist to have Evan's abilities in these areas evaluated. After all, I had gotten a PIP out of her—maybe I was on a roll and could wangle more services for Evan. If nothing else was to come of it, at least I might have learned some techniques for helping him myself.

Naturally, the handwriting specimen that Evan produced for this evaluation was exemplary—his best ever.

Dad, take note; teacher, take aspirins.

THURSDAY'S CHILD

It was going to be a great Thursday. I was back in school after having been out due to sharing one of Evan's colds. The day's agenda listed art class first; an introductory science lab involving powders and crystals was scheduled for after lunch. It was going to be a day that even Evan couldn't fault.

Although he lingered a bit at my desk after entering the classroom, obviously needing to reconnect with me, he soon took off for first-period art.

Missive from Sub
I've never heard that a substitute refused to cover my class, but long epistles from them concerning Evan's behavior always awaited my return. Thus, I was spending my first-period prep time reading the latest one. Evan had been mixing it up when the substitute was in, so she had isolated him by moving his desk to the right of the teacher's desk, near the windows.

When Evan returned to our classroom from art class, he readily sat where I had moved his desk moments before. He was very pleased to find it grouped in the back of the room and next to Jarred, a classmate he admired.

I found that Evan liked to sit in the back of the room where he could spread out his things on two desks, and I liked him at a distance from me. I felt that when he was closer, he monopolized my time even more than he normally did. When he needed to be near me, he would just come up to my desk and sit in the big orange chair, which was right next to mine.

The morning went well, and I knew that my students were extremely excited about the new science unit that I would be introducing that afternoon.

Talk to the Hand
Evan refused to go outdoors during lunch. He decided that he'd rather work on the computer and took it upon himself to go to the resource room instead of following his classmates out to the playground. He was quickly scooted out of there because it was the teacher and her aide's lunch period, too. He then came down to the faculty room to find me. He had been protesting to anyone in authority who would listen that nowhere in

the student handbook did it say that he had to go outside at lunchtime. My colleagues in the faculty room were amused with Evan's protestations and seemed intrigued to see how I would handle this situation. I announced in a voice loud enough so that Evan, who was standing in the doorway, could also hear, that, "I will have to go out in the hall and beat him up."

My curt remark diffused his anger, as the grin on his face indicated.

My beating consisted of giving him a few options:

1. He could go to the computer lab. If the computer teaching-assistant was there, and if she had an open computer, he could stay there until it was time to eat.

2. He could go outside with the other kids.

3. If one or two didn't appeal to him, I could call his father on my cell phone, and he could discuss the situation with him.

He opted to try 1 and 2, and the rest of the day proceeded perfectly.

FRIDAY'S CHILD

The next day was another story. Evan came to school as uncooperative as possible.

After our first-period gym class, Evan climbed on top of the bookcase by the windows and began prancing around, taunting his classmates. Jumping down, he threw over a chair and began kicking male classmates, who kicked him back. He then ran out of the room when he noticed I was heading for the intercom.

I was trying to get through to the resource-room aide for help while at the same time shouting (from my wheelchair) for the boys to leave him be. Yes, Thursday had been a great day, in spite of the hiccup at lunchtime. Would Friday be salvageable?

In spite of my plea, several boys ran after him. They reported back that Evan had run into the principal's office. (The principal later explained to me that in previous years, this had been one of Evan's standard operating behaviors. It was a first this term, though.)

He returned to our classroom with the principal in tow. Evan immediately took charge, pointing out classmates and reporting to her what each one had done to him. When she left, Evan realized that I was furious with him.

I liked to keep and solve problems in the classroom and I never allowed a one-sided diatribe.

When I reminded Evan that the peer-mediation technique "face-off" is SOP (standard operating procedure) in our classroom for solving problems, I could see that he was beginning to realize that by going to the principal, he had been out of line.

NEGOTIATING A BETTER DAY

I then asked Evan if he was ready to cooperate and do things according to classroom procedure. He replied that he was, but only if I rescheduled the second, highly anticipated science lab for before lunch. I agreed, provided that he completed his social studies assignment first. I also told him that I didn't want to hear so much as a peep out of him. Later, as I was setting up the powders and crystals, I again reminded him that we would have the lab before lunch only if he completed his assignment. Immediately, he popped it under my nose.

TGIF

Once again the day was salvaged, and the afternoon wouldn't be a problem. We were studying the Louisiana Purchase and the War of 1812 in social studies, and I could now extend the playing time of Paramount Pictures' *The Buccaneer*[7].

This 1958 movie (tape) certainly brings this historic period to life. Charlton Heston starring as General Andrew Jackson and Yul Brynner playing the pirate, Jean Lafitte, in a story about the Battle of New Orleans, undoubtedly mesmerized my students. (Our school librarian would later correct this and other romanticized film versions about pirates' lives at a special presentation just for our class.)

This unit of study about the Southern states culminated in a Mardi Gras parade. My students wore masks that were begun in art class. Music ("When the Saints Go Marching In") was provided by our instrumental-music teacher accompanied by a few of my musically gifted students, some of whom carried drums. Multicolored beads of all shapes and sizes were garnered for this activity from my niece and nephews, graduates of LSU (Louisiana State University), Loyola, and Tulane. My students

---

7   Anthony Quinn, director, *The Buccaneer,1958*

also threw lots of wrapped candy (hopefully at the feet of other students) as we noisily paraded around the school corridors.

Using all the resources available to enhance the curriculum is my idea of interesting and sound instructional design. My students thought it was just plain fun pretending they were students living in New Orleans at this time of year. As for spending the last twenty minutes or so of several wintry Friday afternoons in the bayous south of New Orleans with those rascals portrayed by Yul Brynner and Charles Boyer, well....

WRITING CALENDAR ASSIGNMENTS

Evan was expected to write every night as part of his homework. The assignment was called "writing calendar" and was based on an idea gleaned from Frank Schaffer's reproducible curriculum materials now being published by Carson-Dellosa. Students in my class were encouraged to do the assignments at home using their computers. I thought this would appeal to Evan. It didn't.

At the beginning of the month, I would give my students a calendar listing a different topic for each night. Some were topics suggested in the Frank

Schaffer material, but I often changed them in order to integrate what was being covered in class. For example, around 9/11 they would be directed to write about heroes. In February, they'd research and write about our presidents. They'd also create different types of poems. (Some of these poems were sent to our war heroes at the VA hospital for Valentine's Day.) In March, they'd write about famous women, the Ides of March, and, of course, St. Patrick's Day.

Formula for Fifth-Graders

In September, my students were required to write only five sentences a night about the assigned topic, but each sentence had to be as long as their age—if a student was still nine years old, the sentence only had to consist of nine words; if the student was ten, then ten words. The sentence-length requirement only changed following their birthday, but each month the number of sentences increased by one. So, by January, my ten-year-olds were writing compound and complex sentences in compositions, which were approximately a hundred words in length; by June that equated to almost a hundred and fifty words.

A *Newsday* columnist said that a career in journalism was foisted upon him when, instead of being expelled from his prestigious Catholic high school, he received a "punishment assignment" that required him to write five-hundred-word essays every night until he graduated. It's amazing how one gets started on his or her career path.

Another writing formula/model, based on input from high school Regents teachers, was given to them for writing DBQ (document-based-question) essays. I learned about this model when I attended a local chapter meeting of the Delta Kappa Gamma Society International. This educational organization enables and encourages teachers to collaborate across grade levels, disciplines, and job descriptions. Membership is worth its weight in workable and inspirational ideas.

PROBLEMATIC REQUIREMENTS

Evan had difficulty keeping up with both the number of words and sentences required. He'd often fall behind and end up having to complete several nightly assignments at once.

Precious Insights

His unique take on assigned topics is noteworthy, and his insights crushingly precious.

On the topic of hurt feelings, he wrote about being "left out" and "the only odd one."

He credited his family as the reason he smiles, and that he tries to smile "at least four times a day." He also wrote that smiling "hurts" so "I don't do it often."

He wrote that he was proud of himself when he got a good note sent home and that on those days, *Newsday's* headline should reflect that fact.

Many topics dealt with friendship. He mentioned that he considered one of the character traits of a good friend to be a sense of humor and stated, "You don't want to be friends with someone mean, do you?" He thought that he was a good friend because he had good ideas for multiplayer games, but lamented that "even so, I still *do* lose some and have very few friends."

When asked in January what he would change about school, he focused on changing the temperature in the classroom to temperate by purchasing a thermometer and installing an air conditioner.

When commenting on how you know when something is right or wrong, Evan stated that you should just "check it, of course," like checking the answer to a subtraction example.

It was "hailing, with a side of thunder and lightning" on his worst day, and there had been a phone call from his teacher. The worst trouble he ever got into was for "touching other people." He reflected on being punished by his dad who took away his electronic game, "which stunk."

He took great pride in recalling how he became the spelling champion of our school. He stated that he was "a little nervous when I was up at the microphone, spelling all of those easy words right, though." He also wrote about being overwhelmed when it came to the semifinals at the college. "I didn't brag after that, because apparently I lost. I can still spell *Antidisastablishmenterianism*. Whatever that means, who cares, but it does mean 1 thing…I know how to Spell."

(Although Evan wrote that he was a champion speller, he misspelled antidisestablishmentarianism. However, I never brought this to his attention. Any ten-year-old who consistently spaces "a lot" correctly deserves to be cut some slack.)

NO TWO ALIKE

It was three days before the Ides of March when I finally began to realize the progress Evan had made.

I was hoping that his parents would allow him to go on a week-long environmental-education trip that was scheduled for later in the year. I knew he'd love it, as it would be chock-full of science activities. His parents hadn't decided, but I had Evan attend the meeting about the trip just in case.

While this meeting was taking place in the all-purpose room, all the other fifth-grade students who weren't going piled into my classroom. Among them was Claudia Jean, who was also diagnosed with Asperger syndrome.

(We had three out of one hundred and nineteen fifth-graders classified with Asperger syndrome. My colleagues suspected that two others were also on the autism spectrum. I can't recall having students medically diagnosed with any form of autism in our school's fifth grade before this year, but then, I didn't teach inclusion classes.)

Claudia Jean wasted no time in coming right up to my face to inform me that I had her brother in third grade and that we hadn't gotten along. Having taught third grade for about a third of my career, I laughingly replied that nobody gets along with third-graders or *me*, and went about setting up the TV to show a film. (Gathering these students together to view a film enabled all the other teachers, most of whom were going on this trip, to conduct the meeting.)

I introduced Castle Rock Entertainment's 1996 film *Alaska*[8] by explaining that part of the story revolved around the survival of a polar bear cub, and that I wanted the students to pay special attention to the magnificent scenery. I planned on stopping the DVD to point out the glaciers as the story unfolded. Since the polar bear is our school's mascot, I believed the children would find this film interesting. I knew Evan and the students in my own class, most of whom were attending the meeting, would have enjoyed it immensely.

Claudia Jean, however, became very flustered by the content and began calling out inappropriately and talking aloud to no one in particular. She became so agitated that an accompanying teaching assistant had to remove her from the classroom. Claudia Jean's inappropriate behavior made me aware of just how far Evan had come since September.

Earlier in the term, Evan would also just call out his opinions, ideas, or comments about a topic.

---

8   Fraser Clark Heston, director, *Alaska*, 1996

A serendipitous occurrence helped me curb this behavior. I had just finished reprimanding him for calling out and made him apologize to the person he'd interrupted, when someone else did it to him. I made an even bigger deal about the rudeness of calling out, reprimanded this student, and made her apologize to him. This seemed to register with Evan, as he had an extremely high regard for fair play, and from that day on calling out still occurred, but less often.

I came to expect Evan to act appropriately when I sent him on errands, put him in charge of something, or brought the class to assembly-type programs. Oh, he could still be a handful, but as the Alaskan film droned on, I could hardly wait for it to be over and for the trip-related meeting to end so that my very own Asperger student and the rest of my kids could return to our classroom.

SOCIAL SKILLS

On the morning of March 30, a mere seven months into the school year, Evan began participating in one of the newly formed social-skills groups.

Evidently Claudia Jean or Kristy (another girl diagnosed with ASD) was in his group. All Evan could do when he returned to our classroom was complain, "Oh, she talks so much and gets so angry when she doesn't win." Indeed.

Because these girls were in an inclusion class, they received help from the regular- and special-education teachers and a teaching assistant. One girl had a personal full-time aide, too. (I was certainly in awe of all the help those two autistic girls received.) I was not told that one or both of them might be in Evan's social-skills group and I was suspicious. Why did the school psychologist set up the grouping this way? Was it in order to have an entourage of helpers nearby in case she needed assistance in dealing with my Evan? Or was I just becoming paranoid?

Around dismissal time, Evan was hanging around my desk. He'd had a pretty calm day, except for an episode of Windexing his classmates when they were cleaning out their desks. I asked him if he was waiting to apologize. His apologies usually included giving me a hug. (I'd been trying to get Evan to understand that fifth-grade boys only hugged their teacher under duress.) So, while he was saying he was sorry, he cautiously looked around before hugging me, stating that he didn't want the other kids to see him.

Did this indicate that my nagging about age-appropriate behavior was finally sinking in? Or was this the precursor of yet another type of storm?

Our Six-Day War

DAY 1 – THE CAUSE

On Wednesday, March 31, our school had a lock-down, or maybe it was a lock-in or a lock-out. Whatever it was, it was as upsetting for the children as it was for the teachers.

Around mid-morning, a quasi-administrator came to my classroom door and told me to close the windows, pull the blinds, and keep the kids in the room. When asked, she refused to give me the reason for doing this, saying, "Why do you need to know?" Seconds later my intercom phone rang. A fourth-grade teacher was on the phone demanding that I, her union representative, find out exactly what was going on. She, too, wanted to know the reason for the lock-down. (She went on to explain that back in 2001, she didn't find out about what had happened on 9/11 until almost noon that day, when a parent came to her classroom door and told her.)

Teachers' Memories of 9/11

The way 9/11 had been handled in our building was unbelievable. Even if a teacher had been told what had happened, she or he was forbidden to mention anything to the students. As children were being pulled out of most classes, including mine, in droves, the ones who were left were imagining all sorts of horrible things. My most intuitive fifth-grade student, lacking all information, thought we were being attacked by the Russians and, like me, kept looking out the windows to see if rockets or planes were coming to bomb us. We weren't ordered to close the blinds or windows that day, which was about the only sane thing that happened.

After reflecting upon the events of 9/11, I swore that I would never again follow an order to lie to my students, even by omission. If the administration wanted, they could bring me up on charges of insubordination for not doing so. I'd rather take my chances for a reprimand and possible dismissal than treat my students with such distain for their intelligence and disrespect for their citizenship. Hopefully, the powers-that-be would remember that teachers must deal in truths and not Orwellian doublespeak.

Extraordinary Measures

So, after listening to the fourth-grade teacher's concerns, I used my trusty cell phone to call our union president to find out what she knew. She in turn made a phone call to a secretary in the central office to find out the reason for the lock-down. (School secretaries know everything; the secretaries in the central office know even more.) She was told that there was a hostage situation involving a police action many miles away from our building, at or near an OTB (off-track betting) site, and that the district was taking extraordinary precautions. As soon as I got this information, I passed it on to both the fourth-grade teacher and my students. Everyone seemed relieved to find out the real scoop.

I believe that, in spite of the explanation, Evan probably internalized this situation as being extremely threatening. He didn't want to go to lunch, and then relented, but first he insisted on accompanying me "safely" to the faculty lunchroom. Although before the lock-down he was able to demonstrate that he had memorized a poem, during and after the lock-down he refused to do any work and appeared agitated.

DAY 2 – THE APRIL OFFENSIVE

Evan arrived at school well aware of the fact that it was April Fools' Day. He could hardly contain his excitement. As I enjoy trying to fool my students on this date, I had loaded the blackboard with lots of items not usually assigned for class or homework. When Evan spotted this, he was delighted. He knew immediately that it was a scam. He got a kick out of seeing his classmates' faces pale when they viewed the amount of work printed there. He had no intention of letting them in on the joke, but finally, to use the kids' vernacular, he "gave me up" when they started to catch on.

When it was time to leave to go to art class, Evan wanted to stay behind with me. About fifteen minutes later, I urged him to go on an errand to the main office with a student who arrives habitually late. I suggested that they both could go from there to the art room, which was in the same corridor. As they were leaving, I reminded them to apologize to the art teacher for coming to class late. (Later, when I checked with her to see if they had arrived, the art teacher was thrilled to report that both verbally astute students had apologized for their "tardiness.")

Problematic Routine Change

Immediately following art class, we had to go to an assembly. Thankfully, this assembly wasn't the usual yelling-and-screaming type of program that some PTA Cultural Arts Committees seem to enjoy booking. The content, designed to highlight the fact that March is Women's History Month, was very appealing to the students. It covered singers and songs that the presenters, who were sisters, said advanced the status of women in the music industry. The largest concentration of the selections focused on modern-day songs and singers. I discovered that Evan and the rest of my students knew almost all the lyrics. As I was sitting next to him, he confided in me that he liked all the songs and singers except for a new female vocalist whom he considered a "wannabe."

When Evan returned to the classroom, it was obvious that all the excitement and the change in routine were having a negative effect on him. He refused to do any work or even to sit at his desk. He was intent on going on the computer so he could play a game—his latest obsession. He put all his energy into trying to convince me that he should be allowed to do so. I held my ground and said he could go on the computer only if he worked a math problem at the board. He refused, but continued standing next to me arguing his point. In desperation I told him he could go on the computer if he participated in what was, by now, social studies time by reading aloud an excerpt from the textbook. He again refused. So I, too, continued to refuse his computer demand, which he restated over and over directly into my ear until it was time for lunch.

That afternoon I knew I should show an instructional film in order to get Evan's attention and focus back. But the assembly had taken up so much time that I just couldn't justify ignoring the work we missed. I had to complete my morning plans for the sake of the other students in my class and try to sneak in some more math. Luckily, Evan became engrossed in something else and didn't continue arguing with me. The afternoon, however, was cut short because quite a few children had to go out to a special chorus rehearsal.

Lost Instructional Time
With the amount of interrupted instructional time that occurs during the school day, it's

amazing that teachers get anything accomplished. Researchers found that 20–25 percent of the school day was "eaten up by lunch, recess, trips to the bathroom, and so on."[9] I'd bet that the "so ons," *no matter how worthwhile,* would actually raise this percentage to far more than 25 percent of interrupted class time.

In the year I had Evan, from March 3 to April 22 (a period of only thirty school days due to Easter/Passover recess from April 5–13), I counted thirty-three interruptions into instructional time in my classroom. The major ones included nine assembly-type programs about the following topics: drug and alcohol abuse, 2; women's history, 1; Jason Argonaut's presentation on Panama, 1; emerging sexuality, 1; author's presentation, 1; Terrific Kids, 2; and Earth Day, 1.

There were twenty-four other interruptions due to the following: bus, fire, and evacuation drills, 4; student trips to the book fair, 3; class meetings about the environmental-education trip, 4; reading celebration/grade-level pizza party, 1; read-in by a community member, 1; extra chorus and musical-instrument rehearsals for the New York State Music Association (NYSMA) competition, 9; jazz band rehearsals, 2.

---

9   Rangell, E.S., Time to learn. *Research Points, 2.*

Not mentioned are the innumerable "normal" daily interruptions caused by PA announcements, intercom calls from the main office, parent drop-bys, and the need to collect things like money and permission slips. Students are also pulled out of class for musical-instrument instruction and reading, math, and speech remediation. In some instances teachers of specific disciplines come into the classroom to provide remediation in their area of expertise directly to individuals in the classroom; called "push-ins," these cause just as much of an interruption.

An Aside
Although the following situations did not directly affect Evan when I had him, they certainly exacerbate the ongoing challenge of maintaining continuity in teaching, and I would be remiss in not mentioning them.

An Insidious Paper Trail
Now the pull-outs, etc., will be noted, as recently teachers were told that they have to *stop teaching* and take official attendance whenever they switch from teaching one subject to another and note where each student is at that precise time.

For example: Students might be working in groups graphing (math) the results of a survey (social studies) and then directed to write an individual report (language arts) analyzing the results. As the integrated lesson progresses one student has to go to a corner of the classroom for push-in remediation, two leave for a violin lesson during the graphing activity, and one student comes back midway into the writing exercise from speech class.

Having to stop teaching and log attendance like this is daunting but may be perceived by both administrators and teachers as necessary because student performance on high-stakes tests is now tied to teachers' evaluations (Annual Professional Performance Review, aka APPR), and missing lessons can definitely impact student performance.

(Following the 2012 massacre at Sandy Hook elementary school in Connecticut, classroom doors in my school district must now be locked at all times—a safety precaution certainly, but having to stop teaching in order to lock and unlock the door each and every time a student leaves or reenters the classroom constitutes more disruptions that must be incorporated into an already slim period of time for teaching.)

Could the need for safety precautions, paper trails, and the like cause an end to multidimensional units and integrated instruction due to time constraints?

In one California school district, similar problems resulted in the formulation of a zero-tolerance policy for interruption to morning teaching time in their elementary schools. The district superintendent reported that this seemingly benign policy caused an uproar because it meant the cancellation of the annual visit of those happy California cows. (Cows only do mornings; they have a great union.)

A Unison Plea

Veteran teachers adamantly reject longer school days and a longer school calendar because we know that extra hours and days will just add more time for interruptions and testing overkill.

Last year New York *elementary* students were subjected to roughly six hundred and seventy-five minutes or eleven hours of state assessments. This figure does not include the hours for students who had to participate in field testing of additional assessments for commercial test-preparation companies. This year *kindergarten* through fifth-grade students will also take an additional state-mandated test in September during the first weeks of school and additional tests in January and April. Not included in the hours for these high-stakes tests are weekly assessments, end-of-chapter tests, midterm exams, finals, and Regents exams.

A Long Island elementary school principal wrote in his welcoming letter to parents that these high-stakes tests, which cost millions of tax dollars, result in a child's being assigned "an insidious" rank as a Level 1, 2, 3, or 4 student. As New York teachers are now being evaluated based on their students' test scores, this principal fears that some children will be less desirable than others to have in class. He feels that this concept is a "blasphemy" as his teachers "live to prepare children to be productive learners and members of society." It is also nonsensical in a school district where 98 percent of the graduates go on to a two- or four-year college.

Teachers are not against a *reasonable* amount of testing or being held accountable. New York State teachers have been held accountable by virtue of Regents Exams since the Civil War era. Twenty years ago (1994) J. Dao of *The New York Times* reported that students enrolled in New York public schools for twelve years took between fourteen and twenty-four criterion-reference tests.[10] Now it seems like students take almost this number of tests in just one year and these tests are not solely based on course material. Parents recognizing the deleterious effect that all this testing is having on

---

10   Dao, J, "New York State is Reshaping Testing System for Schools," *The New York Times.*

children are joining "Opt Out" movements. But even if they refuse to have their child participate in the testing they are unable to prevent their child from having to sit through hour upon hour of "test prep" lessons. The way veteran teachers structure and design research-based lessons and units of study is becoming passé. Now it seems teaching is just drill, drill, drill.

We pray to St. Al Shanker (former president of the American Federation of Teachers) that some-day someone with political clout will champion the idea of an *instructional imperative* so that teach-ers will be able to get back to actually teaching.

Now back to Evan and the fray.

DAY 3 – WEAPONS OF CHOICE

It was the Friday before the Easter/Passover recess. We were going to have a grade-level pizza party, com-plete with ice cream, that afternoon. The ice cream had been added to the menu because my students had met the challenge presented in the Parents as Reading Partners contest—they'd read aloud to their parents for a class total of more than five thousand minutes in a two-week period. It would, under nor-mal circumstances, be a tough day for Evan because of the change in routine and the socializing activity. It became an extraordinarily hard day because of what had transpired on Wednesday and Thursday, namely, the frightening lock-down and the change in routine due to the long assembly program.

Noncompliance
Here is how six hours of noncompliance went on that Friday:

Our day starts out okay. Evan seems to be following the organizational directions given by the aide, Mrs. Lillis. (She had been coming in periodically for about ten minutes early in the morning to help get him set up for the day, which enabled me to give some time to my other students.) Evan completes several early morning assignments, so I allow him to go on the computer.

However, he becomes so engrossed with what he is doing that he doesn't acknowledge or comply with my directive to follow us out to the bus drill. As he usually follows this Mother Duck wherever I go, I don't take notice of his absence right away. While I'm waiting at the door of the bus for the drill to commence, I notice the gym teacher walking Evan out to me. Mr. P. relates that he had been in the hallway near my classroom when he heard unbelievably loud shrieking. Upon entering my classroom, he found Evan staring into the face of the unplugged floor-model fan, which is next to the computer table, and shrieking at the top of his lungs. As Evan could have easily looked at the daily agenda, which was always printed on the board, to find out where we had gone, he wasn't about to get a doting reaction from me. I order him onto the bus and thank the gym teacher, who gives me a look of profound sympathy as he walks away shaking his head.

Missing Pencils

Upon returning to class, Evan notices that the two girls who sit on either side of him are moving his desk forward. (The nighttime custodian had pushed their desks too far back.) Before we went out for the bus drill, I had asked the girls to help me move his desk forward along with their own, as Evan was totally absorbed working at the computer station. When Evan notices that they dropped some of his colored pencils on the floor, he goes ballistic.

He not only accuses them of dropping the pencils on purpose but also of stealing two of them. He begins smacking the girls on their arms until I wedge my body in between him and them. He continues ranting in spite of the fact that most of his classmates now are looking for his missing pencils. Thoroughly exasperated, I threaten to call his dad. Evan usually will do almost anything to stop me from calling him, and again this ploy works well. He begins to calm down, but he refuses to do any work, including taking the weekly spelling test, an activity at which he excels.

Things couldn't get worse, right? But, they do.

To Eat or Not to Eat?
During lunch period, Evan comes to the faculty room door where in a very loud and bitter voice he complains to me about the adult lunchroom monitors. He says that they are insisting that all the fifth-graders sit quietly at their tables, in spite of the fact that no one is going to be eating right before the pizza party. He thinks that this is "idiotic." He feels that the students should be having a longer play period outside. So do I, but I explain that I'm not in charge of the lunchroom.

Creamed!
When we return to the classroom, he handles the pizza-and-soda part of the party okay, but when the ice cream is served, he loses it. Evan doesn't like whipped cream, but as soon as he sees the shaker can of it, he grabs one and begins squirting it at anybody within his reach. It is at this particular moment that

Valarie's grandparents arrive at my classroom door. They want to wish the children and me a happy Easter and to pick up their granddaughter for early dismissal. They can't believe what is going on as they watch me dive out of my wheelchair to retrieve the whipped cream can that Evan is wielding. The class mother, whose daughter Brittany is always well behaved, also looks stunned and doesn't know how to help me with this situation.

Losing the whipped cream can to me, Evan fills an empty plastic bowl with some melted ice cream and tries to dump it on the head of any classmate within his reach. When some lands on Matthew's head, he cries until he realizes that I am easily cleaning off his hair with a paper towel. When Evan decides to pour the rest of the bowl on his own head, I order everyone to sit down immediately. I isolate Evan by making him sit in the orange chair next to my desk.

Caned!

It was then that I notice Charles crying. He tells me that Evan hit him in the stomach with my cane. How had I missed that? I immediately send him with a sympathetic classmate to the nurse's office and keep Evan in check at my desk. Minutes later when the intercom phone rings, I know that it's the main office calling. The school secretary says that the principal wants to see Evan immediately. Evan, however, does not intend to comply with this request. He remains seated in the orange chair and watches his classmates as they clean up the room.

Windexed!

Unexpectedly, Evan lunges for a squirt bottle of Windex that is filled with soapy water. Grabbing it, he begins spraying it at anyone in his vicinity. I motion to Andrew, who is nearest to him, to retrieve it. As Andrew reaches for it, he slips on the soapy floor and falls on top of Evan. With that, J. T. and Caleb pile on top. Evan is now "mortally wounded" and refuses to get up from the floor.

I warn Evan that he is not to move out of the orange chair or touch the squirt bottles of Windex, which he so loves using and abusing.

After a while, Evan asks me why he wasn't allowed to help in the cleanup. I sit down next to him and relate all the things that he shouldn't have done, especially using my cane as a weapon. He replies that he doesn't recall picking up my cane, much less hitting a classmate with it.

Thank God for the miracle of the dismissal bell and for the cease-fire that the Easter/Passover recess provided.

DAY 4 – BACK TO THE BATTLE FRONT

The war was not over.

The cease-fire during spring recess did little good except for giving me some R & R. Upon returning to school on April 14, Evan presented me with a letter from his father. Dad had not read my report of what had happened until that morning. In his letter, he urges me not to hesitate in calling him when Evan is in the midst of a meltdown.

His letter made me feel better, but he only knew about what had happened Friday morning with the bus drill and pencils. I hadn't the energy or inclination on the Friday afternoon following the class party to write about the whipped cream, caning, or Windexing incidents. I had just wanted aspirins—lots of aspirins.

On Saturday, April 3, I had called Charles's parents to see how he was doing and to find out if he had given them any more information about the caning incident. Charles's father explained that his son understood that Evan couldn't always control himself, but he was afraid that at some point, his son was going to fight back. He emphasized that his son was capable of hurting Evan.

More Aspirins Please

Evan wasted no time in letting me know that things had not improved.

After handing me his dad's letter, he said he was hungry. Instead of walking to first-period art class with his classmates, he took out his lunch, plopped it on the table next to my desk, and began eating it. I was not sure where this was going, so I let him continue. Perhaps this would give us some quiet time to talk together. No, Evan didn't want to engage in a two-way conversation. He was just interested in enumerating all the things he wanted me to let him do before he would comply with any of my directives.

It was going to be another Excedrin day.

However, in the afternoon I got Evan to participate by assigning him a demanding role in a play based on a Sherlock Holmes mystery. Evan the actor could never turn down a good role.

DAY 5 – ALMOST THE FINAL FRACAS

Evan persisted in being uncooperative and noncompliant. Assignments continued to be ignored.

Snail Mail

When this happened, I usually sent Evan's unfinished work home through the mail. His dad would see to it that assignments were completed. Thus, I had sent home a packet containing many uncompleted assignments on April 1, the Thursday before spring recess. Evidently this packet of work didn't arrive at Evan's house until Thursday, April 15—two days after the end of the recess.

That night, his dad had him complete many of these assignments. Those not completed, he had to finish in the morning. As a result, he arrived at school on Day 6 "loaded for bear"—I being mama bear.

DAY 6 – ASPERGER SYNDROME: 6; TEACHER: 0

Alea iacta est! Indeed, the die had been cast. Evan was furious that his dad made him complete all his assignments. He knew he wouldn't get any sympathy from me on this subject, but he was going to rant and rave anyway. He announced that he wasn't going to our first-period gym class, but I was having none of that—at least not at nine o'clock in the morning. After some hemming and hawing he went, and when I checked with the gym teacher, I found out that he did participate, although grudgingly.

A Chaotic Meltdown

When he returned to the classroom, he was worse. He sat down in the orange chair and began shredding my copy of *Newsday* with a magnetic letter opener[11] that I keep attached to the front of my metal desk drawer. He began vociferating about how unfair his dad had been and that I wasn't to give him any more homework—not ever. As he continued his tirade, I wasn't sure if he knew where he was or what he was doing or saying. He was in complete meltdown, and I knew we both needed help.

Unfortunately for me, I had left my cell phone in my car, or I would have called his dad immediately. I tried calling the school psychologist on the intercom, but she didn't answer. I called the main office looking for her, but I was told that she and the principal were in a meeting with a parent and couldn't be disturbed for any reason. In desperation, I called the resource room looking for Mrs. Lillis. After hearing what was transpiring, the resource-room special-education teacher, Mrs. J., rushed down to my classroom. When she saw Evan's state, she said she would watch both Evan and my class while I went to get the psychologist out of her meeting and phoned Evan's dad. We both knew that

---

11   The letter opener was very sharp but designed for safety.

I was the one who needed to leave the room, as so much of what Evan was angry about, in his opinion, was my fault. She then went to sit as close to Evan as possible.

Although Evan kept shredding the newspaper, I gave him a directive before I left. I wasn't sure if he would be able to focus on what I was saying, but I told him that he was to stamp his classmates' agenda books. I was hoping to lessen the intensity of the shredding behavior. Evan can easily handle more than one task at a time, and rubber-stamping the books where classmates copy the daily schedule, class work, and their nightly homework assignments is a job all my students relish; having him concentrate on more than one activity might help bring him out of meltdown, I thought. It was worth a shot.

Later, Mrs. J. reported that Evan did stamp the books as his classmates brought them up to him, thus interrupting both his shredding behavior and his outbursts. But in between the stamping, he continued shredding and raving until he ran out of newspaper.

Failed End Run
Evan's dad was not surprised to hear from me—he knew Evan was obsessing about the homework when he'd left for school that morning. I asked him

to please come and pick Evan up. He said he would do so readily, as he realized the situation must be pretty bad; I had never made such a request before. However, to return from where he was presently working would take him a long time. We had to come up with another plan.

When I returned to the classroom, I told Evan that I had called his dad, and his dad wanted to speak to him on the phone in the nurse's office immediately. By now sufficient time had passed, enabling him to comply with this directive.

As I glanced at the mess on the floor that Evan had made of the newspaper, I must have sighed aloud. When I stooped down to begin cleaning it up, one of the boys in my class, J. T., immediately put up his hand to stop me, saying, "I'll clean it up for you." I could have kissed him.

For Better or Worse; in Sickness or Health
Evan told me that after he talked with his dad and the psychologist, he was sent to work in the resource room with Mrs. Lillis. She kept him there until it was almost time for lunch. He then went to sit at his desk in our room, but did nothing. Following lunch, he was back at my desk demanding that he not be given any homework that night.

Evan was scheduled to attend another meeting about the environmental trip later that afternoon. My colleagues were not happy with the idea of taking Evan along, and based on what had transpired in the last six days, I was beginning to agree. Misbehavior on his part at this meeting would certainly lead to his exclusion. I told him that if he behaved and paid attention at the meeting, I'd cancel one of his homework assignments, but that wasn't acceptable to Evan. I was to cancel all of them, and I was to do it before he went to the meeting. No, I told him. I would cancel one assignment, but only after he had proven he could behave. I held my ground, hoping there wouldn't be another outburst. Finally, Evan relented and went to the meeting. When he returned, he immediately had me cross out an assignment in his agenda book. I wrote on the side of the page that I canceled the assignment because of his good behavior at the environmental-trip meeting. Upon reading what I wrote, Evan lost it. He angrily scratched out what I had written, saying that his dad would make him do it when he read that it was part of a deal. I was too exhausted by this time to care anymore—whatever.

SURRENDER!

Asperger syndrome had beaten me, but there would be no relishing of victory on Evan's part and no agony of defeat on mine. Evan's parents would see to it that his medication was adjusted or changed, and we'd just begin anew with *tabula rasa*—a clean slate.

CHAPTER 12

Staking My Reputation

A CHANGE OF ENVIRONMENT

As alluded to in preceding chapters, fifth-grade students were eligible for a week of outdoor educational experiences at a forested mountain site about three hours away. The trip for our school was usually scheduled for the first week in June. Planning for this trip, however, began in March. Only fifth-grade students and teachers who volunteer could go—no parents. Not every student decided to take advantage of this opportunity, which cost the students in Evan's class approximately three hundred dollars. (A portion of the total fee was paid by our regional BOCES—Board of Cooperative Educational Services.)

When I asked Evan if he wanted to go on the trip, he immediately answered, "Of course." However, he wasn't sure if his parents were going to allow him to attend because of "all the medication I have to take." I didn't think twice about writing to his parents, urging them to consider his participation. When I didn't hear from them, I brought it up in a phone call with his dad.

PROS AND CONS

I told Dad that I thought Evan would love it. As there wouldn't be any pencil-and-paper tasks, I thought there would be little reason for Evan to become argumentative. He would surely enjoy working on all the environmental investigations. I didn't think that canoeing, orienteering, or even the cooperative-type games would present a problem. I knew from past experience that the naturalists explained activities in great detail and wouldn't stand for anyone being left out or refusing to participate.

I also knew that all but two of the boys in my class slated to go genuinely liked Evan. I would get them all to promise me that they would look out for him; I would translate this for them as meaning "give him his way" if things get dicey.

WORST-CASE SCENARIO

I shared most of this info with his dad. He agreed with my assessment but still had concerns. I told Dad that if Evan couldn't handle it, he would get a phone call from the teacher in charge (as I wasn't going) asking him to take Evan home.

I knew that having to drive a long distance to pick up their son wouldn't upset his parents. They'd recognize that whatever Evan got out of the trip would be well worth any inconvenience. But it was their decision to make. I urged them to attend the upcoming parents' meeting, which would provide information on how medication and other details were handled.

ALIENATING COLLEAGUES

When my colleagues discovered that Evan might really be going on the trip, they were furious with me. Why was I urging his attendance when I wasn't going? I told them that I believed Evan would do just fine; if he didn't, his parents were very willing to drive up and collect him. I did request that he room with Jarred, as Evan would follow his lead. The teacher in charge thought this was a good idea, but when it came time for the kids to be paired up, Evan chose another student with whom nobody else wanted to room. When this boy's mother found out that her son would be rooming with Evan, she was so upset that she came to school to complain to the principal. Her son was also a student who my colleagues felt did not belong on this kind of trip.

To be fair to my colleagues, I must state that this trip placed a tremendous amount of responsibility upon them. They are wonderful teachers, but taking children with special needs and complicated behaviors to a site so far from home was daunting. They would have felt better about taking Evan if an aide accompanied him. The fact that so many children took different medicines added to their stress. A nurse at the facility dispensed some, but not all, of these medications. The teachers were responsible for administering the remaining dosages after the nurse left for the day. (Each year, they loudly lamented this situation, wishing that the nurse could be there for a longer period.)

TRIUMPH!

The pairing, however, seemed to be set in stone. In the end, it worked out well. I can only surmise that it worked because the two boys related to each other intellectually; both were extremely intelligent.

When I inquired about how things went, my colleagues told me that Evan did pretty well. They also related that he lost his water bottle when they arrived and wouldn't consider using any other, even though they went out and bought him a new one. Instead, he insisted on drinking water only from the paper cups in the medical office.

When I spoke to Evan's parents about his successful participation on the trip, they were beaming. "We didn't get one phone call about him."

CHAPTER 13

Conduct Unbecoming

SEXUAL URGES

When Evan realized that he had been a handful, he'd come up to my desk at the end of day and lay his head on my shoulder. This was easy for him to do, as I was spending more and more time each day teaching from a wheelchair borrowed from the nurse's office. He'd then apologize and give me a hug—an endearing behavior, but, as mentioned previously, not age-appropriate for a fifth-grade boy. This was just one of his many unseemly behaviors that I was attempting to address.

Evan's body contact with mine was becoming more pronounced. This was accompanied by the open use of licentious language. Evan even announced to the class one day that he was going to shove a pencil up his butt, gleefully stating that it would get all chocolaty and then he'd eat it. When I contacted his dad about these kinds of inappropriate remarks, he told me that the same thing was going on at home.

His dad said that he spoke about my observations and concerns with Evan's doctor. The doctor felt that they were another aspect of the syndrome. I wished that his doctor had to deal with all the angry notes I imagined would be forthcoming from the parents of my other students about Evan's crude remarks. (I am still amazed that I didn't get any.)

By fifth grade, "potty talk" exists on a subdued level. Sexual remarks are more common. They are usually limited to a specific gender group and revolve around emerging boy/girl interests and the changes taking place in their bodies.

Once again, Charles was the only one who seemed particularly upset with Evan's words. "Would he really do that to himself?"

ANOTHER DR. PHIL?

I envision a fulfilling career in psychotherapy for this sensitive, caring young man. Or was I just observing in Charles the reaction of someone worried about his friend? Evan certainly liked to mix it up with Charles. Was physical interaction the way this autistic boy attempted to forge a friendship? I hit you—you hit me back—we're friends. Had Charles recognized and accepted rough touching as a sign of Evan's friendship?

Touching certainly plays a role in emerging love relationships. Looking back at Evan's other physically abusive interactions, it is obvious that the same set of students (Valarie, Matthew, Anna, and Charles) were involved again and again. In Evan's mind, did they represent his circle of friends?

STEPPING OVER THE LINE

It was after a long day of serious conflagrations when Evan's attempts at apologizing for his actions went awry. Those actions included but were not limited to: using foul language in the lunchroom; touching Charles's butt while he was working a math problem at the board; and hitting classmates with my long pointer. When I had tried to call for assistance, Evan pulled the cord out of the phone's handle and attempted to shove me and my wheelchair into the hall, away from the intercom.

Thus, at dismissal time he was all over me, pleading and demanding that I not call his father. Because of what had happened earlier, I asked Mrs. Lillis to come in ahead of time to help with Evan. While she was packing up his materials, Evan suddenly jumped onto my lap and, while hugging me, he pulled the clip on the back of my bra.

SHELL-SHOCKED

Had he been a young teenager in upper-middle or early high school, the impulse to do this to a girl in his own age group certainly would be considered inappropriate but not unheard of. Dr. Freud and others might even rationalize that this behavior for young males is understandable—the old "boys will be boys" mentality. I was, however, the teacher and authority figure in the classroom, and no matter how strong sexual urges are for a ten-year-old boy or how nurturing a teacher is, this just doesn't happen—at least it had never happened to me.

I was stunned and moved my wheelchair away from him, standing up in the process way taller than my almost five-foot height actually allowed. While looming directly over Evan (rather like a wicked queen in a Disney movie), I told him in no uncertain terms that this was unacceptable behavior. I stammered that I was an adult and his teacher—how dare he?

Realizing that I was more than just a little upset, Evan quickly put on his backpack and darted out of the room.

Did he remove himself from the situation because he understood that his actions were inappropriate and because he was embarrassed? I doubt it. I believe he left because he knew I was irate. Remorse for his actions was a common reaction; embarrassment over them was something I had never observed.

I was still standing, discussing the incident with Mrs. Lillis, when one of my younger colleagues passed my room. Observing my agitation, she came in to find out what was going on. I was still so dumbfounded that I just blurted out what had happened. All she could do was shake her head while commiserating with us. She and Mrs. Lillis asked what I would do. "Call Evan's dad," I replied, which I did.

The next day Evan entered the classroom as if nothing had ever happened.

CHAPTER 14

Field Trips, Food, and Forces beyond Control

EATING ISSUES

I had encouraged Evan's participation in the environmental-education trip because in the past, I found him to be a pleasure to take on field trips. He viewed them as interesting, participated willingly, and had always been well behaved.

In the fall, we had gone on a large charter fishing boat to explore the sea life in the Great South Bay. Evan's only complaint on this trip was that his dad had fixed him two sandwiches to eat. At that time there were still control issues about food, which seemed to have been carried over from fourth grade and home. Two sandwiches in Evan's opinion were "two *too* many." I suggested that he eat just half a sandwich, as the sea air tended to make one hungry. "Not me," he replied, and he went on to whine a bit about food.

I learned that I needed to give control of problems like the sandwich issue over to Evan. He needed to come up with the solutions. In many ways my elderly mother was like this too. She often said she just wanted to talk about her problems—she didn't want my solutions.

Evan's eating issues soon became nonissues because I allowed eating in class. He interpreted this to mean that he could eat whenever he wanted, and the food issues in school, and later on trips, just evaporated. Eating in the classroom, of course, has a side effect—ants—but the kids in Evan's class delighted in observing them. They enjoyed setting up pathways and seeing which of their crumbled chips or pulverized snacks the ants preferred. I've been told, though I don't necessarily subscribe to the dictum, that every class should have a pet. Ours became the ants. (When we attended The JASON Project telecast later in the year, my students and I were flabbergasted and then intrigued when one of the scientists featured—a man working in the field in Panama—explained that he too was investigating the behavior of ants.)

POSITIVE INFLUENCES

On our first field trip, I made sure Evan had a partner to sit with on the bus, but as the year progressed, that was no longer necessary. The kids picked up on my philosophy that everyone needed to be included. They knew I didn't want to see anyone eating, playing, or sitting alone. Evan, however, really preferred sitting alone and I allowed it on the return trips to school when he was tired.

LUCKILY, A NO-SHOW

Evan didn't go on our second field trip to the Cradle of Aviation Museum as he had been there before and felt that he had been cheated by the gift shop cashier. His parents wisely kept him home that day.

STRIKE UP THE BAND

When we went to hear the Long Island Philharmonic Orchestra, the seat designated for the teacher was at the opposite side of the row from Evan. Although I didn't anticipate problems, I wanted to be nearer to him. By moving a few students around, I was able to sit closer. Evan then changed his seat with one of the boys so he could talk to me about the binoculars he had brought. Nobody except the ushers seemed to mind the swapping of seats. As the program was about to begin, though, Evan complained that he couldn't see. I asked him how he could solve this problem. He said he wanted to return to his original seat. Therefore, I asked J. T. to change back, which he did readily, although I saw "the look." When J. T. plunked down in front of me I whispered, "Thank you," so that only he could hear me. His annoyed look changed immediately into a smile and nod. During the performance, I saw the boy on Evan's right pretend to conduct the orchestra, but Evan shook his head at him, and they both continued to sit quietly and listen to the fantastic music.

A FRANK FINALE

Our last class field trip was on June 2 to a Broadway show. Evan's dad had some apprehensions about letting Evan go to a theatre in New York City. The ticket for a nosebleed seat was expensive (about ninety dollars) but included chartered bus transportation, which had to be purchased in March. Evan had yet to demonstrate how well he could handle the environmental trip (June 7–June 11), and I wasn't sure if I would be attending the show, since the date for my orthopedic surgery hadn't been set. Eventually, I was able to convince Dad that Evan's past behavior on trips indicated that he would be fine. Fortunately, I was able to attend, but I was unable to introduce Evan and my other students to the show's musical director, a former fourth-grade student of mine. (He was out of the country at the time working on another project, for which he won an Emmy.) Evan, a few other kids, and I commiserated about this as we wolfed down "dirty water" hot dogs on the bus trip home.

CHAPTER 15

The Play's the Thing

EAST OF BROADWAY

Plays made up the lion's share of my reading program. I found they worked well not only for teaching reading skills but also by providing cross-subject integration. Fortunately, Evan usually loved reading and performing in plays as much as the rest of the kids in my class did.

Plays are highly motivational, and when every student is assigned a role, there is no problem keeping their attention. No one is left out because extra character parts can be written in as needed or the narrator's role divided among several students. Plays give students a lot of practice with on-the-spot decoding, reading aloud, and listening for cues.

My students also used the opportunity plays presented to create a character's personality by changing the way they phrased their lines or by emphasizing individual words. Sometimes a student created an accent for his or her character. This usually led me (and the rest of the class) to convulse with laughter.

I never had a student unwilling to participate in reading a part in a play. They also knew that if it was the first read-through, "messing up" was okay.

When he read aloud, Evan's voice often sounded whiny. Frequently, his intonation and inflection were flat, so I would criticize his voice for not being in sync with that of the character's personality or mood. Evan the actor was very open to this kind of criticism and tried to adjust the tenor of his voice accordingly. If he didn't have a substantial part in the play, however, he'd just tune it out after delivering his lines.

EMERGING SHAKESPEAREAN TROUBADOURS

My students often took plays on the road. That is, they would work in small groups to polish a play based on a popular book or a significant historical figure or event. (They even tackled an abridged version of a play by Shakespeare and stories, in play format, by Arthur Conan Doyle, Charles Dickens, O. Henry, and de Maupassant.) Then they went around the school knocking on classroom doors, inquiring as to whether the teacher would like them to put on their play for the class. Sometimes teachers signed up in advance for such performances. Our presentation of *You Are There: The Hanukkah Story Brought to Life* by Milton Polsky, a play about the first Hanukkah, became a seasonal classic in our public school. (However, with today's embedded journalists in war-ravaged areas, my more recent students no longer viewed having TV reporters at the scene of a battle that took place in 167 BCE as bizarre.)

Evan took turns being either a cast member or the director of an acting troupe. Sometimes his being in charge didn't go as smoothly as I would have liked, but no worthwhile learning or leadership activity is without risks.

THERE'S NO BUSINESS LIKE SHOW BUSINESS

Therefore, it wasn't surprising when Evan nailed the lead in the annual spring play. This play about our community's development was staged and presented, complete with abbreviated costumes, in our classroom.

Overcrowded conditions coupled with the lack of respect for dramatic arts in our elementary school meant that using the school's stage was out of the question. Our stage, located in the all-purpose room, was used three periods a day as a cafeteria and the remaining periods for instrumental-music lessons, chorus rehearsals, PTA meetings, professionally produced assemblies, etc. There was little opportunity for students to practice or present plays there.

Second-graders came to see rehearsals in our classroom at different times during the week, as this play enhanced their study of communities and local history. (They were a terrific audience.) Parents, siblings, relatives, community members, and local politicians were invited to an evening performance, which was also staged in our classroom. Each year, so many people attended this performance that the audience overflowed into the hallway. This presentation usually coincided with our school's celebration of the Parents as Reading Partners program and the statewide school-budget vote.

MONKEY BUSINESS

This relative of old-time Tammany Hall politicians found that if you want to turn out positive-minded voters for the school budget, just present a play performed by children a few steps down the corridor from the voting machines. It's downright devious electioneering.

APPLAUSE, APPLAUSE

Evan was marvelous as the lead in our play, having easily memorized his and everyone else's lines. Yes, this is the same kid who couldn't memorize fifty state capitals for the social studies tests. (Maybe "wouldn't memorize" should be the operative phrase here.)

At the conclusion of the play, when he pushed his 1940's fedora-style hat from the back of his head down toward his nose—*a la* Frank Sinatra—Evan brought down the house.

CHAPTER 16

A Novel Approach to Fear

THE MISSING "BOOK" REPORT

I wish I had read Mark Haddon's empathic novel *The Curious Incident of the Dog in the Night-Time*[12] the year I had Evan. I learned so much from it after the fact.

Haddon's main character, Christopher John Francis Boone, is a bright, "behaviorally challenged" boy who, at every turn in the story, must face, meet, or overcome fear.

---

12   Haddon, *The Curious Incident of the Dog in the Night-Time.*

Through this simple tale, I believe that Haddon enables the reader to enter the mind of an autistic child. Embedded are many of the realities and idiosyncrasies associated with autism. It resonates with his character's black-and-white, literal, egocentric worldview. Christopher need not be thought of as a composite of many different individuals, even though the author may have created him that way. Christopher is so like my real-life Evan.

One glaring difference was that Evan hated math, while Christopher excelled at it. The author underscored this fact by numbering chapters in sequential prime numbers and by having Christopher sit for his A-level exam in math. Evan excelled with words and "sat" for the semifinals of the spelling bee at our local community college. Thus, to me, even in their differences, their attributes and abilities were parallel.

Haddon's presentation of the cornucopia of fears that Christopher had really makes me wonder about the approach I took with Evan. If I had read Haddon's book before having Evan in class, would I have concentrated harder on trying to allay those fears rather than focusing so much of my time and energy on his behaviors?

I knew things would go smoother when I was able to walk Evan through an activity and help him anticipate events and situations. Oh, I guess I could blame not being able to do so more often on lack of time or additional adult help. But I think because I knew Evan was so bright, I thought he would be capable of dealing with his fears better than he actually could. I am not a fearful person, so I tend to negate its impact on others—especially bright individuals. I knew my gifted students worried about things like the Earth moving out of its orbit or the sun shutting down. As we have no control of such things, I usually dealt with their fears in a very cavalier fashion. I imagined that Evan had similar fears. I recognized early on that Evan needed to be in control, but it wasn't until I read Haddon's book that I understood that, like Christopher, Evan's view of so many ordinary situations as being uncontrollable, was terrifying.

Thanks for the insight, Mark. And I'm sorry, Evan—please forgive me for not doing better.

CHAPTER 17

"Gaudeamus Igitur" and "All That Jazz"

A FINAL "WORD"

When I began teaching, graduation from elementary school was called step-up day. It wasn't supposed to be a big deal. The big deal was supposed to come when students went from eighth grade to high school. But change it did. Now elementary school graduation to middle school is also full of pomp and circumstance.

Although I was scheduled for major orthopedic surgery on June 7, I promised my students that I would attend their graduation ceremony on June 23 if I was physically able to do so. Fortunately, I was able to return to school on the morning of their graduation and keep my promise.

Each fifth-grade teacher made a brief speech at the ceremony. I usually included in mine information about the various career paths that all our fifth-grade students hoped to pursue. I enjoyed emphasizing the usually overwhelming percentage of those who planned to become teachers. Minutes before the ceremony, I scanned the yearbook to find this information. I was struck by the fact that one girl had chosen "herpetologist." Missy, who was standing with the group of girls surrounding my wheelchair, wasn't sure what it meant. Evan, who was standing on the periphery of this group, nonchalantly replied, "Oh, that means she wants to work with reptiles." No one doubted that he was correct. Evan's classmates always accepted every piece of factual information he contributed as accurate. Once again, I marveled at the wealth and scope of his knowledge.

Tempus Fugit

Evan had a banner year. He passed all state and district tests, including a "killer" of a math test designed by a middle-school math chairman to make children fail. It included far too many items not found in either the fifth- or sixth-grade math curricula. (According to the math chairman, the purpose of this test was to weed out those who didn't belong in an accelerated math class in middle school. He could have just asked the teachers. Instead, he made the teachers angry and several female students cry. Before this test these girls felt confident about their mathematical ability.)

Having won the spelling bee, Evan had represented our school in the semifinal competition at our local community college. And he had been the star of our class play.

But the accomplishment that made me the proudest was when I would see Evan occasionally work his way into a small group of students who were quietly talking, laughing, or giggling together.

I also had a banner year. Evan had allowed me to be his teacher, but more importantly, he had become mine.

Bite, Jump, Run!

A PROBLEM IN MIDDLE SCHOOL. REALLY?

About three weeks into the next school year, a few of my former fifth-grade boys dropped by to see me after school. When we finished catching up, I asked them if they knew how Evan was doing. Almost in unison they exclaimed, "You haven't heard?"

According to the boys, it was sometime during the first or second week of school that Evan bit one of his new teachers, jumped out of the classroom window, and ran home.

No, I hadn't heard about any of this, but I would. As soon as they left, I phoned the middle school and left a message for a teacher with whom I had previously worked to please call me.

AGAIN IGNORING HISTORY

All of the fifth-grade teachers had met a few weeks before graduation with the social worker and the principal of our middle school for an articulation session. The original purpose of this type of meeting was to prepare the middle-school staff to receive our elementary students by fostering an informal, collaborative chat. I believe both sides thought the now-mandated "chat" was a colossal waste of time.

When I attempted to tell the middle-school representatives about Evan's needs and added that he might need special placement, the middle-school principal put up her hand to stop me from speaking. In a very condescending tone of voice, which I could barely hear, she told me that *their* guidance counselor would establish his program. As I endeavored to add information about his outrageous behaviors, the social worker smiled smugly and said in the same low, condescending tone that they'd had students like "what's-his-name" before and were very capable of dealing with them. He wouldn't present a problem.

Indeed.

Their calibrated tone of voice as well as their know-it-all attitude certainly demonstrated that they did not want my input. After all, what could I, a mere elementary teacher, possibly know?

THEIR UNIQUE SOLUTION

When my former colleague returned my call, although evasive, she confirmed most of the boys' story. She added that following this incident Evan was immediately classified, given an IEP, assigned a personal, full-time aide, and placed in *her* self-contained special-education class.

SO ELUSIVE, YET SO SIMPLE

Although I never would have recommended that Evan be placed in the restricted environment of a self-contained classroom, I wish I had known that a mere "bite, jump, and run" were the required prerequisites for getting an extremely bright autistic boy classified as a student in need of special-education services. Evan the actor, his classmates, and I could have staged that in a New York minute.

Glossary

Asperger syndrome is defined by the CDC (Center for Disease Control and Prevention) as one of the autism spectrum disorders (ASDs). "Although symptoms are present early in life, Asperger syndrome is usually diagnosed when a child is school aged.... [T]he brain of someone with this condition functions differently than that of someone without Asperger syndrome.... People with Asperger syndrome have problems with social, emotional, and communication skills, as well as unusual behaviors and interests." (http://www.cdc.gov/ncbddd/acte-arly/pdf/parents_pdfs/Asperger_Syndrome.pdf)

Attention-deficit/hyperactivity disorder (ADHD, aka **ADD)** is defined by the CDC in the following way: "People with ADHD have trouble paying attention, controlling impulsive behaviors (might act without thinking about what the result will be), and in some cases, are overly active." (http://www.cdc.gov/ncbddd/adhd/)

Autism per se is not defined on the CDC website. Instead, it links and defines it as one of the autism spectrum disorders (ASDs), which is "a set of complex neurodevelopment disorders that include autistic disorder, Asperger disorder, and pervasive developmental disorder not otherwise specified…. Children who have ASD display mild to severe impairments in social interaction and communication along with restricted, repetitive, and stereotyped patterns of behaviors, interests, activities…. CDC's Autism and Developmental Disabilities Monitoring (ADDM) Network revealed a 78% increase in ASD prevalence between 2002 and 2008….Based on parent reports, the prevalence of diagnosed ASD in 2011–2012 was estimated to be 2.00% for children aged 6–17. This prevalence estimate (1 in 50) is significantly higher than the estimate (1.16%, or 1 in 86) for children in that age group in 2007." (http://www.cdc.gov/nchs/data/nhsr/nhsr065.pdf)

Individualized Education Plan (IEP) comes under the Individuals with Disabilities Education Act and is defined by the CDC as "a legal document that lets the school know what kinds of assistance will be needed by a child during the school day. An IEP is created by parents and school personnel, such as a psychologist, teachers, a school nurse, and a physical education teacher, as well as any other professionals that **parents** think might be helpful." [emphasis added] (http://www.cdc.gov/NCBDDD/spinabifida/school-age.html)

504 Plan is required under Section 504 of the Rehabilitation Act of 1973, which is widely recognized as the first civil-rights statute for persons with disabilities and paved the way for the 1990 Americans with Disabilities Act.

The CDC defines a 504 Plan as follows: "If a child does not qualify for an IEP, a parent can request a 504 Plan be developed for their child at school. Usually, a 504 Plan is used by a general education student who is not eligible for special education services. By law, children may be eligible to have a 504 Plan, which lists accommodations related to a child's disability. The 504 Plan accommodations may be needed to give the child an opportunity to perform at the same level as their peers. For example, a 504 Plan may include the child's assistive technology needs, such as a tape recorder or keyboard for taking notes and a wheelchair accessible environment." (http://www.cdc.gov/NCBDDD/spinabifida/school-age.html)

Bibliography

Blumberg SJ, Bramlett MD, Kogan MD, et al. Changes in Prevalence of Parent-Reported Autism Spectrum Disorder in School Aged U.S. Children: 2007 to 2011–2012. National Health Statistics Reports; no 65. Hyattsville, MD: National Center for Health Statistics. 2013. Accessed June 13, 2013. (http://www.cdc.gov/nchs/data/nhsr/nhsr065.pdf)

Center for Disease Control and Prevention. "Autism Spectrum Disorders (ASDs)." Accessed June 13, 2013. (http://www.cdc.gov/ncbddd/autism/index.html)

Dao, James. New York State is Reshaping Testing System for Schools. *The New York Times*. May 1, 1994.

Haddon, Mark. *The Curious Incident of the Dog in the Night-Time.* New York: Vintage Books, 2004.

Ozonoff, Sally, Geraldine Dawson, and James McPartland. *A Parent's Guide to Asperger Syndrome and High-Functioning Autism: How to Meet the Challenges and Help Your Child Thrive.* New York: The Guilford Press, 2002.

Paulsen, Gary. *Hatchet.* 2nd ed. New York: Simon & Schuster, 1996.

Rangell, E. S., ed. *"Time to learn." Research points*, 5(2) AERA, 2007. Accessed June 13, 2013. http://www.aera.net/Portals/38/docs/Publications/Time%20to%20Learn.pdf

Rock, Gail. *The House Without a Christmas Tree.* 2nd ed. New York: Alfred A. Knopf, 1985.

Taylor, Sydney. *All-of-a-Kind Family.* 3rd ed. New York: Dell Publishing, 1989.

The JASON Project: JASON Education through Exploration. Accessed. June 13, 2013. http://www.jason.org

Acknowledgements

Marilyn (Mimi) Whitehouse's wisdom

Geri Brown's acumen

Janet Marcley's editing

Jaclyn's IT expertise

Kim's medical knowledge

Brett and Gina's "Kindling"

Samantha, Brett, and Matt's savvy

Salee Jean's computer program guidance

Allan A. Glatthorn's inspiration, literally from on high

Jennifer Klump's REL evidence-based research

Penny Ellis's special-education facts

Charlie Kick and Eileen Arnow-Levine's cyber print knowhow

David Ruetschlin's stamina

Richard Gavila's shopping around

Janet Baram, Joan Carroll (UK), Maureen Daddona, Victoria Danay, Carolyn Fredericks, Maxine Geller, Marie-Louise Nordesjo (Sweden), Rachel Shapiro, Vivian Sheperis, Maria Toulas, and Gloria Wilson's insights

All of the Alpha Phi (NY) Chapter of the Delta Kappa Gamma Society, International members' camaraderie

David Abalos, Irene Abrahams, Dave Arneson, Eileen Erikson, Rosemary Pace, Mary Roane, Joyce Tang, and Trisha Ventker's encouragement

The Children and Reference Librarians' mega resources and personal knowledge

ACKNOWLEDGEMENTS

CreateSpace editorial and design team's infinite patience

And most especially Sal, keeper of the hearth and my heart

Any errors, assumptions, or conclusions, however, are mine alone.

Available for purchase at Amazon.com, Kindle,
www.createspace.com/3799797,
and other online retailers

www.meandthataspergerkid.com

Made in the USA
Columbia, SC
23 March 2022